# WINNING AT
# REMOTE
# WORK

— · —

## SUCCEED ON YOUR TERMS FROM
## ANYWHERE

## SHAWNA WING

# CONTENTS

# Introduction

It's 2022, and the world has changed quite a bit in the past couple of years. With the onset of Covid-19, a worldwide pandemic, we all experienced a disruption to our daily lives that included working from home, children learning at home, having groceries and other items delivered, talking to grandma over Zoom during the holidays instead of seeing her in person, and wearing masks, just to name a couple of things.

Although the first couple of months during the pandemic were stressful, we adapted to the new norms in our lives. And one of those new normals was working from home.

Picture it: You were at home in your most comfortable pair of pants and sipping coffee from your favorite mug. In one moment, you are watching Netflix from your laptop. A few notifications later and you change tabs to report to your boss from halfway across the world as you maneuver to your home office to dig into work.

You perform the tasks given to you and you are done within half a day. Once your workload is done, you can decide to finish off where you left off on Netflix just a few hours ago, complete another set of tasks from another employer, exercise, take your dog to the park, or even start a load of laundry.

A decade ago, such a scenario would either be rare or downright unheard of depending on who you were talking to. However, remote work has not only become a possibility nowadays but a necessity for a new generation of workers who want control over their schedule, their priorities, and their workspace.

Working remotely, for me, was a personal dream. The ability to work for anyone anywhere across the world without having to relocate myself has always intrigued me. However, I never thought it was going to be a possibility until I read about people called "Digital Nomads".

Like the nomads of old, these people ventured into uncharted digital territory and paved a trail for everybody else to follow. Sure, some of these people are not millionaires, but they were able to successfully prove a concept and work on their own terms. They managed to realize their dream while forging a path for the rest of us.

Sure, trying out a new concept is never going to be easy. I had no idea what I was getting myself into most of the time when I began my remote work journey. However, with enough research, trial, and error, I was able to find a system where I can make more than enough money by remotely working.

Being part of a relatively new and uncharted business model is great. Why? This means that there is no set path, no one-size-fits-all solution that will help you earn money. The solution that worked for some might not work for you and vice-versa. But eventually, you will find that remote working is a whole lot better than being stuck at a desk at some office for 8 hours straight (not counting a commute that keeps you away from other priorities like family and hobbies as well as sitting in a car that increases greenhouse gases).

In this book, I have laid out the path I took to working remotely and becoming my boss. Everything will be included here, especially the challenges I encountered and how I managed to deal with them.

It's been years since I decided to completely change to a remote working setup and I am still reaping its benefits. What I enjoyed here is the freedom, flexibility, and agency that help you achieve your goals without spreading yourself too thin. In time, I know you will also enjoy those benefits and more.

Without a doubt, the remote work setup is the future! The technology to work from absolutely anywhere is already here. It's up to us to capitalize on these advancements for our gain. And if you are the one that is eager to embrace the future, I suggest you turn to the next page now and start reading.

Good luck on your own journey and have fun!

**1**

# THE BASICS OF REMOTE WORK

When you tell someone that you're a remote worker, things can get murky quickly. Does that mean you work for a company remotely? Does that mean you are a freelancer and work with various clients of your choosing? Are you a contract worker? Or an entrepreneur with your own business? All of the above? Or none of the above?

So, before we get into the nitty-gritty details in the rest of the book that outlines the steps needed to rock the freelance world, we're going to go over some basics. Don't worry. The concepts are not particularly complicated to understand. However, it would still be better if you have a general grasp of how things work under this setup before you try to apply it to your situation.

Along those same lines, it is an excellent idea to determine if you are compatible with remote work. A self-assessment at the end of the chapters in this book can help determine if you're suited to remote work. Throughout the book, the assessments will also give you an idea of any adjustments and preparation you will need to undertake as you transition out of the office. Finally, the self-assessments will outline the steps you need to take in order to successfully maintain your freelance life.

So, are you ready to jump in?

## What Exactly is Remote Working?

In the broadest sense of the term, <u>remote working</u> is any type of work that is done outside of a traditional office setting. This can include working from home, working from a co-working space, or even working while traveling abroad.

To truly understand this definition, you must remember that the typical work setup in the twenty-first century now is composed of three elements.

First, there is the employee or worker (i.e. the one that must perform tasks). Second, there is the task or set of goals that must be accomplished. Third, there is the environment or a place where the tasks must be accomplished under specific, time-bound conditions.

Remembering those elements, remote working simply proposes a question: is it really necessary for a person to be bound to a specific, time-constrained work environment to be paid for the performance of tasks? Every proponent of this setup and digital nomad would answer you with one big NO.

Advancements in technology have increased the convenience and exchange of information between companies and private individuals. Content can be made on almost every device and then immediately sent out to the entities commissioning their creation. Also, communications can be set up anywhere so as long as the native internet connection allows for it.

What this means is that the necessity for the conventional workplace has significantly diminished. Teams meet over Zoom to brainstorm for the new account, share ideas via online apps and workspaces like SLACK, and communicate easily through email. Technology (and the pandemic) created a new work/life balance, and workers loved the ability to work from home offices, (thereby eliminating that pesky commute time as well as wear-and-tare on vehicles and helping the environment), and spending more time with their families. For example, Alisha, an accountant for a large corporation, discovered that she can work earlier in the morning when she is most productive (instead of going into the office at the standard 9 A.M.) and free up more time to cook, exercise, and work on her hobbies in the afternoon when she would've been stuck in traffic or still at work.

As of this writing, 26.7 percent of U.S. workers are fully remote and projections show that remote work continues to climb globally, ever after the pandemic. Seventy-six percent of employees believe that remote work offers a better work/life balance and are happier, as well as better for the company- remote workers get up to 40 percent more work done remotely than in a cubicle.

As we continue to reimagine what the post-pandemic work world looks like, more remote and hybrid options are opening up that benefit both companies and employees. Some standard

9 to 5 jobs are here to stay and might re-surge in importance the more that the world recovers from the pandemic.

However, the events of the most recent years have proven that remote working is a viable setup and might be the superior alternative- especially if we continue to find that remote workers are more productive.

## History of Remote Working

The truth is that the Remote Work experience started in the late 1970s, right at the dawn of the computer age. In 1973, the term "Telecommuting" was coined by NASA engineer Jack Nilles to describe a unique work agreement where an employee does not need to show up at work to do their assigned tasks.

In 1979, IBM allowed 5 of its employees to perform all the tasks they were given right in the comfort of their own homes. There was no special setup or agreement done here. These 5 people were just told to do what they usually do for five days a week but in a place other than their usual workplace cubicle. All that they have to do is to come up with the desired output to get paid.

Five years later, the number of people working remotely under IBM's employment rose to 2000. Other companies like JC Penney followed suit and allowed some of their staff to work from home.

Have you heard the term "start-up"? By the late 1990s, college students rented out garages as rudimentary office spaces where they can work on their newly-formed businesses. Of course, these were temporary setups as they only helped their owners prove their concept. Eventually, a lot of these "garage startups" were able to get backing from investors and became successful brands. Amazon, Apple, Google, and even the toy manufacturer Mattel started in a garage.

## The 2010s and Recently

As of 2010, it was noted that the population of remote workers has exponentially increased by 400% since 2001. At the same time, more companies are designed to be "remote-first" while other companies were becoming "remote-friendly" (we'll discuss more of this later). Sixteen percent of companies are fully remote, with more companies following suit.

In the past decade, the issue that drove remote working to the forefront was the matter of employee wellness. In essence, companies were becoming aware of how the conventional workplace setup was no longer conducive to the well-being of a lot of employees. During the late 2010s, it was IT companies like Google pushed for the allowance of more employees to work from their homes. For some companies like Twitter, however, remote working was not an option but the only available workplace setup.

And then the pandemic happened. The outbreak of COVID-19 in late 2019 and early 2020 forced a lot of countries to implement lockdowns. This meant that a lot of conventional workplaces were left unattended for months to a full year.

At the same time, the need to produce output while also earning enough money to make ends meet remained at a high. Thus, remote working no longer became an option for many workers but a downright necessity.

And for those whose employment was terminated by the pandemic, two options were given. The first is to find a job that allows for remote working. The second is to set up their own online business. The latter option allows for a greater agency but provides its own set of risks.

What this means to say is that a lot of people today embraced the remote working concept not because it is an option for them. Instead, remotely working or running a business is the only way for them to earn money while the rest of the world waits for the pandemic to blow over.

## What Does Remote Work Bring to Companies?

Assuming that the pandemic did not make remote work a necessity, what does the concept bring to the table as far as employees are concerned? Keep in mind that no company will ever try something out, even ones that benefit the worker, if it does not help their bottom line.

So, here are some of the benefits that companies can get if they embrace remote work, completely or partially. These are good benefits to bring up if you ever propose a remote work setup to your boss; make sure you lead with how much it will save money for the company as well as benefit them in other ways.

## Cost-Saving

The costs involved in managing a collective workspace for employees can become expensive for companies. The primary concern here is rent as real estate has become expensive in recent years. And even if the company owns the lot on which the office is situated, there are other costs to consider including the following:

- Utilities

- Maintenance

- Cleaning

- Furnishings

- Equipment repairs and replacements

- Emergency costs (such as repairs in case of fire, earthquakes, floods, and other unexpected events).

With remote working, the company can save money by letting people work in spaces that they have full control over. There is no need to provide them with expensive equipment as they can do so for themselves. Also, any downtime due to repairs or equipment failure is costs no longer attributed to the company.

## Employee Morale

Even if the company provides its employees with the most exciting, regulation-compliant workspace out there, there will come a time when their motivation to work in that same space for years will decrease. The problem here is not the office itself. It is just that the human mind's willingness to do something tends to decrease the more repetitive the scenery or the action is.

This is why a lot of companies invest in vacations, sick leaves, and constant office renovations but these can become costly for them in the long term. With remote working, the company allows its employees to do their tasks in an environment where they are most comfortable.

And if they don't feel comfortable in that place anymore, they can easily relocate to another space without incurring costs for the company.

## Wider Talent Pool

If there ever was one huge advantage that remote working gave to a company, it would be outsourcing. Allowing for remote working removes the issue of limiting your candidate search to one city. Employees don't even have to be local relative to the company just to work for them.

And then there is the matter of training costs which are reduced or completely removed with remote training. It is easier to find specialized people now without having to train them from the ground up. Of course, the need to relocate employees has also been greatly reduced or removed with remote working.

## Time

With remote working, time is more efficiently used. No longer do employees have to wait for a few minutes or an hour for people to commute, punch in, and get to their workspaces. A day in the company can start in a few seconds as everybody logs in to an online-based system.

This also removes the limitation of a company having to work only 8-hour shifts. Depending on where employees are located, the chances of the company being available 24/7 have increased.

## Loyalty

By allowing an employee to be where they are most comfortable, the company builds rapport with them. What many companies are starting to understand now is that many employees quit not because of low salaries. They quit because they work under management that does not seem to care about their well-being.

Offering a remote option sends the signal that the company trusts its employees enough to produce the output required of them without overbearing monitoring. And when employees

feel trusted and appreciated, the company will be able to retain
them for a few more years. This saves the company a lot of time,
effort, and money in training replacements.

## Productivity

As odd as this might sound, many employees tend to be more
productive when they can remotely work. This is because their
need to be as comfortable and in control is already provided.
Thus, what is left is for them to do their tasks as efficiently as
possible to receive payment.

## But What About You?

So what does remote working bring for you? Here are some of
the benefits to expect when you embrace this work setup.

## Freedom

In as much as you are bound by your contract, you still want
to have a little bit of freedom over how you do things at work.
You'd rather not want your work to dominate every single aspect
of your life no matter how much you need your monthly salary.

With remote work, you can get to make work a part of your
schedule and not THE single task you must perform for everybody above everything else. There is enough flexibility here to
let you do your tasks while still attending to your concerns.

As a remote worker, you can get to have a medical checkup, go to sporting events, attend recitals, and bond with your family while still meeting your daily quota. And since you are in control over your time, you can get to do equally productive things for the rest of the day (we'll talk about this in a later chapter).

## Optimizing Expenses

The very act of showing up at work can get expensive. You need to pay for gas, food, clothing, and other necessary expenses just to be there from 9 am to 5 pm for 5 days straight. At the same time, you need someone else to take care of your children for the day while you are out at work.

But since you will be at home, all of those costs can be reduced or removed entirely. A meeting is being called at 3:30 PM? Just click on the chat invite and turn on your camera. Are the kids making a ruckus while you are working? Just head to the next room and spend a minute or two with them.

With everything within your reach, you won't have to pay an extra dollar just to attend to all your concerns, professional or otherwise.

## More Time

Remote working allows you to better manage your time. If you want, you can do all your work in the afternoon while you attend to personal matters in the morning. Or you could work in the evening and sleep in the morning.

Whatever the case, remote working helps you perform in conditions where you are the ablest to do your tasks. So as long as you do not inconvenience the rest of your co-workers and still meet deadlines, there is no stopping you from doing your tasks according to your schedule.

That being said, being in control of your own time requires you to be as consistent as possible in following a schedule. There is the danger of becoming too comfortable with your free time. Avoiding this pitfall will be discussed in detail in a later chapter.

## Mobility

With a remote setup, there is the ability to work everywhere you like. You are no longer bound by guidelines that require you to show up at an exact spot and stay there for hours until your shift is over.

This also removes the usual problem that comes with relocating. For instance, your family might want to move to a new city or state. A remote work setup will stop you from worrying about having too far of a commute or resigning from the company.

## Peace

Not all people can deal with the typical noise or fluorescent lights coming from an office. The buzz of telephones ringing, people talking, and cars honking in the street can be an auditory assault for some. At certain points, all that noise can become unbearable and prevent you from taking focus.

If you are the type of person that is at their most creative when everything is quiet, then a remote setup will work well for you. Being at your own home means that you can control the noise levels in your workstation.

Sure, you are not completely removing workplace noise. You are just replacing the typical noise from the office with the ones at your home. However, a remote working setup allows you to drown out all the unnecessary ambient sounds so you can focus on the task at hand.

## Protecting Your Health

If work is currently stressing you out, you can turn everything off and take a rest. You can then return to the task at hand once you have given your mind the rest it needs

And, of course, being happier means that the output that you produce tends to be of better quality. A constant stream of good output will open up more opportunities for advancement (and increased confidence) later on which can make you happier.

## The Stigma is Gone

Back then, remote work was seen as that odd setup best given to shut-ins and other maladjusted yet competent workers. If you want to work remotely, most of your co-workers will think that you are strange, unprofessional, or lazy.

As of 2022, many companies have had to find a way to do their tasks remotely. As such, the stigma of having to resort to remote work is no longer there.

## Better Work-Life Balance

By being in the same place for an entire day, the theory is that you should have better control over your work and your life. For example, since you no longer have to commute, you can have more time for a healthier breakfast.

However, the most important benefit of a remote work setup is that it frees up more of your time. You could use this time to improve your skills, tend to personal concerns, or find another job/sideline to complement your current income.

## Control Over the Workplace Environment

At home, you have full control over the setup of your workplace. If you can tolerate a bit of clutter, you can maintain such a workplace and no one will complain.

If you want to decorate your space with action figures and plushies, you can do so and no one will think that you're a nerd for it. And if you love to keep things tidy, you have full control over the cleanliness of your space, and no one else will be there to ruin it for you.

This setup also allows you to create an environment that is conducive to your productivity. If you are the one that functions well while listening to music, you can blast your favorite tunes while working and no one will complain. If you love to watch some YouTube videos from time to time for a break, you can do so and come back to your work with a clearer head.

The point is that the home is the perfect place for you to set up an office space without having to worry about the judgment, back sass, or ridicule of others. Whether it is rudimentary, untidy, or professional-looking, that remote workspace will most definitely reflect you.

## One Last Thing Before You Proceed...

At this point, you should realize that a Remote Work/Business Setup will help you in more ways than one. It won't matter if you want to embrace this concept fully or just want a part-time setup at home.

A remote work setup is here to help you set up a work environment that is conducive to both your productivity and well-being. Even if there was no worldwide, lockdown-causing event, the advancements in technology would still make this setup more of a possibility for a lot of workers right now.

And this does beg the question: what is out there for a worker like you? You'd be surprised at how many remote working or business opportunities are just waiting for you to take advantage of.

But before anything else, you should get yourself armed with the right kind of tools and skills to qualify for any of the jobs in the market.

# Chapter One Action Steps

**Take the time to journal about the following questions...**

- What type of Remote Work are you interested in? Why?

    ○ Remote Work as a full-time employee

    ○ Remote Work as a contract employee

    ○ Remote work as a freelance employee

    ○ Entrepreneurship

- If you are a full-time in-person employee wanting to make the change to remote work, time to start putting together a remote-work proposal for your supervisor.

    ○ Questions to address in your proposal:

        - Why you would be a good candidate for remote work

        - How this will save the company money

        - How this would benefit the team and company

        - What hours do you plan on being available for your team

- Are you willing to try a probationary period?

- Are you willing to try a hybrid (some days in the office, some days remote)?

- Taking the leap into the remote world can be daunting, so make a list of the benefits that you looking forward to as a remote/freelance/entrepreneur.

  ○ What appeals to you? What would you be willing to fight for to have a better future?

    - More control of your time?

    - More control over your environment?

    - More productivity?

    - More creativity?

    - Flexibility?

    - Less time stuck in the car or commuting?

    - Better work-life balance?

    - Better for your physical, mental, and emotional health?

    - Better for the environment?

# 2

---·---

# SO, I THINK I WANT TO WORK FROM HOME...

W hen Covid hit, Jenna was initially excited to work from home. She set up a workspace in the corner of her large bedroom, started attending meetings in pajama bottoms and slippers, and sipped her favorite coffee brand all day long. Not having to commute was nice, and she realized that the extra time without the travel allowed her to spend more time reading and writing. She even started a couple of new hobbies that she had always been meaning to get to but never had the time for, like making homemade pasta and drawing. It was nice...at first.

And then the honeymoon ended. Jenna missed dressing for work, seeing her co-workers and friends, and even going out to lunch on Fridays at her favorite brick-oven pizza place. As an extrovert, Jenna felt deprived of human connection at home; for her, Zoom wasn't enough facetime with her department. As a creative, Jenna craved the time spent chatting with co-workers and brainstorming on projects informally while they were working in a collaborative space. She started to get annoyed by her desk, monitor, work calendar, and whiteboard in the corner of her bedroom because as she lay in bed at night her gaze naturally fell to that side of the room and all the tasks that she needed to get to the next day would flood her thoughts.

While working from home she was distracted by tasks that needed to be done around the apartment, like laundry and dishes; she missed the clear boundary between work and home. So, when her boss offered her the option of remaining fully remote in the fall of 2021, Jenna turned it down. She felt that remote work wasn't the right choice for her.

Chances are you got the chance to dip your toes into the remote world during Covid. Transitioning into remote work takes the right mindset, skills, organization, and drive to make it a fulfilling choice.

## The Pros and Cons of Working Remotely

Working remotely for most corporate employees is a dream come true; you can finally have the work-life balance that you have always wanted. You're not stuck in traffic, doomed to horrible coffee, or obligated to listen to your co-worker's endless tales about her new Shih Tzu puppy. The crazy office politics or gossip doesn't bother you anymore, and you're more productive because Dave isn't constantly dropping by to interrupt your spreadsheet flow with the same questions he asks every day. It is a dream come true.

The work-from-home setup benefits us in more ways than one. For instance, it gives us the freedom to work at our own pace, in our own time, and in our own space. Bosses will not be able to micromanage us; co-workers will not bother us. We can also take care of our loved ones while still being productive at work. Food prep and delivery services have also become more popular, making it easier for us to get our meals without having to leave the house.

On a positive note, working remotely means having enough time to raise our children with more intentionality. With both parents working from home, they can easily take turns in looking after the kids. There are also more opportunities to do things that we enjoy like taking a break to play with our pets or going for a walk in the park. We can use our lunch break to run errands or take a power nap. Parents working at home may have more time to tutor their kids. This may lessen the expenses of after-school classes and other enrichment programs. Even monitoring their studies is easier and more enjoyable.

Moms with infants or toddlers may have a hard time adjusting to working at home. It can be quite challenging to work and look after a baby at the same time. The same goes for employees who have elderly parents or sick family members that they need to take care of. They may find it difficult to juggle their responsibilities at home and at work. Employees who are used to working in an office may find it hard to transition to working remotely. They may not have the proper setup at home or they may not be able to focus with all the distractions at home. For instance, kids running around or pets that need attention. It can be quite challenging to find a balance between work and life when you are working from home and parenting.

On the other hand, we can also save a lot of money by not going out as often. We no longer have to buy new clothes and other materials for work or spend on gas for our vehicles. We can cook our meals at home and pack our lunch instead of eating out. If we are careful with our spending, working remotely can help us save a lot of money in the long run.

Working from saves us from traveling long hours just to get to work. We can use that time for other things like spending time with our families, doing errands, or taking a break. It also allows us to work in our most comfortable clothes and in our most relaxed state. We can take as many breaks as we want without having to feel guilty about it. For commuters, working from home can save them a lot of money in the long run. With the cost of gasoline and vehicle maintenance, working remotely can help us save a great deal of money as well as help the environment. Also, we don't have to face crowds and traffic.

Some workers bought gym equipment and fitness gadgets to use at home during the pandemic; working from home can definitely lead to better fitness and health. For example, we can also use our lunch break to walk around the neighborhood or do some stretching exercises.

While others find it difficult to adjust to the "new normal," others find it healthy for their workspace ergonomics and postural setup. A study from the University of Stanford found that people who work from home are more productive than those who go to the office. They also take fewer sick days and have fewer distractions during work hours. A stronger workflow rhythm can be one pro from working remotely.

On the flip side, working remotely can also be a source of stress and anxiety. We no longer have the support of our colleagues when we need it. Working remotely can be quite lonely and isolating. Others may be left out due to the absence of social interaction. We also tend to overwork ourselves because we feel that we need to prove our worth to our bosses. With no clear boundaries between work and life, we can easily get burned out.

Others find it difficult to adjust to working from home. Like Jenna, some workers thrive on collaboration and human interaction or need a very concrete boundary between work life and home life that working at an office or on a job site offers. Some workers do NOT want to take work home with them or have space in their homes that are devoted to their job.

Saving money from staying home can be a pro or a con, depending on how you look at it. If you are the type of person who is easily tempted to spend, working remotely can be quite dangerous for your finances. With all the delivery services available and the ease of online shopping, we can easily find ourselves spending more than we should. It is important to set a budget and be mindful of our spending when working from home.

Mental health is a downside of working remotely can be one of the most difficult to manage and cope with. In a study by Harvard Business School, they found that employees who work from home are more likely to experience "ambient belongingness threats." This means that they feel like they're not really part of the company even if they are. They may feel isolated and alone which can lead to anxiety and depression. It is important to find ways to connect with our co-workers even if we are not physically present with them. We can have video calls, join online communities, or simply reach out through social media.

## Why the Right Mindset Matters

The key to successful remote work or entrepreneurship is knowing yourself. Do you work best alone, with others, or in a mix? Do you like to collaborate? Can you focus on one task at a time without getting distracted by your environment? Do you have a space at home (or in your community, like the library or coffee shop) where you can focus on work? Are you good at organizing tasks and managing your schedule? Can you prioritize and meet deadlines?

As a remote worker, everything has been arranged in your favor. What do I mean by this?

You're already working in a place that you like, at a pace that you prefer, and with jobs that meet your skills. You have full control over your time, the people that you meet, and the tasks that you complete every day. With almost everything stacked in your favor, the only thing that can prevent you from earning money with remote work or business is, well, you.

## Essential Skills

Once you have the traits of a good remote worker, you can start focusing on the skills needed to succeed as one. Sure, every remote work out there has its own set of required skills. The skills below are more general in the application which means they will become vital to your career as a remote worker and not just for one particular job. If you develop these skills, you'll be able to work remotely for your entire career!

Here are some of the skills that every remote worker or digital nomad should have.

## Time Management

Being the boss of your own schedule has its downsides. Chief among these disadvantages is the potential to become lax with your work time and procrastinate. Thus, the ability to stick to a schedule without anyone telling you so is crucial here. Are you good at keeping yourself accountable?

For instance, if you are a worker that is at their best-performing tasks from 9 am to 5 pm, then you must make sure that you are already at your workstation a few minutes before 9 am. This also means that every other task not essential to your work must be done before or after the shift. Jenna knows that she performs best on an 8-4 schedule, and likes the structure of the full workday. Tomas, a remote worker from Spain, splits his time, and works from 8:30 - 12:30 and then 2:30 - 6:30. In the afternoon he enjoys a long lunch and walks his dog.

This does not mean that you should stick to one schedule at all costs- this is an upside to remote work! Rachael volunteers at her son's school once a week and makes up the time on other days. Jake lives on a farm and has occasional power outages that result in unintentional downtime. These are all things you can take into account with remote work.

And if you do meet sudden changes in the plan, you have two options. One, you can find a place where you can resume work as soon as possible. Two, you can switch allotments so the tasks you ought to perform now can be done later and the tasks to be done later can be done now.

Either way, you have to keep yourself accountable to a schedule.

## Self-Motivation

With nobody to monitor you, you also run the risk of becoming unmotivated to complete your tasks. Thus, your ability to motivate yourself is a crucial skill in this field of work.

The ability to self-motivate requires you to understand how your mind works. Questions to think about as you move to remote work are:

- What motivates you to complete work before a deadline?
    - Breaking it down into pieces?

- ○ Having someone check your work?

- ○ Rewarding yourself with _____ (fancy coffee, exercise class, etc.) when the task is complete?

- ○ Checking it off a list?

- What are your workplace preferences?

  - ○ Do you like to have a supervisor looking over your shoulder?

  - ○ Do you like to collaborate with co-workers?

- What can distract you?

- Which of your goals drive you towards completing your tasks?

- What behaviors do you have that prevent you from finishing your work?

If you are distracted working at home, plan on spending part or all of your workday in a coffee shop, library, or other work-spaces. (I personally love working at my local library. We have a small historical community room with a large table and couch. I don't get distracted by tasks at home, and I get out of the house when I need to. Better yet, I can walk a couple of miles there and back, getting exercise.)

These are just some of the questions that you can ask yourself to find out how to keep yourself productive during the day. And despite what the name implies, you can always ask for the help of others to motivate yourself. A strong support system is as crucial in remote work as any skill or equipment.

## Organization

Having little supervision means that you have to do everything yourself. Organization revolves around how you manage your projects so they are finished on time and professionally (i.e. not at the last minute). For example, content writers follow a content creation schedule that tells them what to do for that day and what needs to be submitted.

How will you organize your workflow? Will you keep a digital schedule or a physical planner? When will you schedule meetings with clients so that they best fit into your project schedule? Krista, a full-time copywriter who works on websites for small businesses, only takes meetings on Tuesdays. Since her job involves a lot of focused creative time, she doesn't want to stop at random times when she is in the flow of writing to take a meeting. Tuesday is the only day that she is on Zoom; that does, however, mean she will sometimes have four hours or more worth of meetings with clients on Tuesdays. With a lot of trial and error, she realized that this was the optimal production schedule for her business.

Organization also involves the physical setup of your workplace. Do you have a dedicated space within your home to work or will you have to constantly move around because your partner is using the desk or the kids are watching TV? Where is the place in your home with the least amount of distractions? Do you have enough light? Plugins for your computer and printer? Good Zoom access? The good pens and a notebook? Work manuals or a drafting table or several computer monitors? Do you have an area where you can both sit or stand at a desk? Regardless of your style, everything that you require to do your job must be within your arm's reach.

## Communication Skills

Remote workers are good communicators, period. They respond to emails promptly, they contribute during Zoom meetings, and they share on online workspaces like SLACK regularly. And all of this communication is organized/time-managed into their day (Ahem, see above).

A crucial communication skill you can develop here is the ability to get to the point ASAP. For instance, can you tell a co-worker without having to deliver an entire preamble (but without being rude)? Can you make an argument without needless elaboration? If the answer to both is a yes, then the chances of people quickly understanding what you mean are high.

As someone who creates his/her own schedule, you don't want to waste time typing a saga over email when five sentences, including the greeting and closing, would do.

## Teamwork

The majority of remote workers are still members of a team, working collaboratively and communicating about a project in order to produce the best results for a client. Teamwork and communication go hand-in-hand. Jenna, the remote worker from the beginning of the chapter, had a couple of teammates who were laid off from the company for the following reasons: they didn't respond to emails within 24-48 hours, if they came to Zoom meetings they never contributed verbally or in the chat nor did they ever turn their screens on, and they stopped meeting important deadlines.

We've all had co-workers who didn't follow through- and it was soooo frustrating. The same is true for a remote worker. If you drop the ball, the project can't move forward and your coworkers are going to avoid working with you on future projects.

One crucial lesson you must learn here is accountability. If assigned to a project with multiple people, you should at least produce output on time. Also, keeping your team informed of your progress is a crucial habit you must form.

## Tech-Savviness

The modern iteration for remote work requires you to be as comfortable with technology as possible. Some jobs like SEO and Internet Marketing even require you to be constantly updated when comes to trends and current events to be competent. As for most jobs, you only need to be familiar with some remote work applications. These programs are collaborative and will require you to learn how to perform file transfers, communicate via chat, and send e-mails to the proper parties.

Each job will have its own set of programs and tools that you must be familiar with. Although these tools will be covered during the training period, it would be preferable if you can learn how these programs work for yourself. YouTube is your friend when trying to learn a new app or program.

Lastly, you need to be familiar with some job or tech-specific lingo. Some specialists do talk using these terms exclusively. If you want to know what the rest of the team is talking about, you should learn their distinct language first.

## Emotional Intelligence

In the past this was called the "ability to read a room". Remote work setups require you to be as perceptive as possible when communicating as you only have audio and visual cues to rely on.

A strong emotional intelligence helps you form the proper responses to questions which can help in facilitating smooth communications. At the very least, it can help you avoid conflict and solve problems.

A strong emotional intelligence will also require you to be as aware as possible of your idiosyncrasies. How do people react

to your presence? Are they comfortable whenever you talk or
engage with them? Try to be as mindful as possible of all the
verbal and non-verbal cues people give to you on the screen and
adjust your behavior accordingly. At least, this can prevent you
from getting yourself into truly awkward remote interactions.

Note: If you have noticed by now, all of these skills cannot be
developed overnight. Some are honed through years of practice.
Others through deliberate assimilation into one's daily habits.

Either way, you can only develop these crucial skills if you
consciously apply them daily. You can also look at various online
resources on tips to apply these skills to your daily life.

## Essential Tools

With your personal qualities sorted out, the next thing to look
into is your assets. Regardless of the job you will get hired for,
every remote worker out there has to have access to a set of tools
that will make their jobs all easier.

Here are some of the hardware and software you should invest in to be effective in whatever remote work you take on.

## A Working Desktop or Laptop

Without a doubt, this is the most important asset you can invest
in for remote work. You can either go for a desktop PC setup or
a more mobile laptop setup. Desktops are ideal as they usually

have better performance than laptops. On the other hand, laptops are cheaper and are mobile by design.

Tomas uses both a laptop and a desktop depending on if he is working at home or out and about. Selena, due to the nature of her job, needs to have multiple monitors in order to work as a CPA because she needs to have tax codes, spreadsheets, and other items up at the same time for reference.

## Ergonomic Chairs

Your sofa or dining table chair might be great to sit on for your work but they can be bad for your back in the long term. This is because they are so comfortable that they won't allow for an upright sitting posture for hours.

What you should be looking for is an ergonomic chair that features lumbar support to hold your lower back. Some adjustable levers for the chair and arm height are also neat along with some tilting. In essence, you should find a char with enough adjustability to let you work on a comfortable yet healthy posture for hours.

Also, consider a desk or space that allows you to both sit and stand while working. Selena, the CPA I mentioned, invested in an adjustable computer stand that sits on top of her desk. As someone with back problems, she stands for part of her day and sits for the rest, engaging different muscles.

## Ergonomic Keyboards

While we are on the topic of ergonomics, you should also consider the keyboard that you will be using for your work. Aside from having all of its keys functional, the keyboard itself should offer proper support for your wrists to prevent joint problems and the dreaded carpal tunnel syndrome.

Look for a keyboard that offers wrist support at the sides for both left and right wrists. This way, your hands will not be aching from the strain after a long day of work.

## Whiteboard and Sticky Notes

A good trick in productivity is to never let your brain do all the remembering. Whenever you have tasks that need to be completed, have them written down on something and placed at a point that you can easily see when glancing away at your monitor.

You can buy a whiteboard for a few dollars at your local store and have it placed just above eye level in front of your workplace. Something across your desk or above a wall will be the ideal mounting point for your whiteboard. Dan, a creative who works remotely from a home office, just uses sticky notes as reminders and puts them on the back of the door, which is in his line of sight. He likes this because when the door is open, no one else can see the messy jumble of sticky note reminders, but as he is working, he can see the reminders or tasks out of the corner of his eye.

You can also use sticky notes as little reminders at the side of your screen. The purpose of these tools is to help you remember and visualize your goals so you could finish them as quickly as possible.

If you like a reminder tool that goes with you, consider getting a planner or using a digital planner. Digital planners can link to your google calendar; some workers find it easy to go back and forth digitally while working online.

## Other Essentials- nice to haves...

The following items are not exactly needed to complete your remote tasks. However, they do help in making your workspace all the more conducive to productivity.

## Plants

More than just for aesthetics, plants can help in filtering the air while also giving your workspace a lighter feel. They also have this strange ability to help you manage your stress by providing you with some positive energy to focus on your work. A study has shown that workspace productivity increases by 15% if you were to introduce plants to the vicinity.

Of course, you need to take care of the plants so they can continue providing some positive vibes to your workspace. Some succulents are ideal for this situation as they only need water once or twice per week.

## Noise Canceling Headphones

For those who cannot focus if assaulted by a lot of noise, there is the option to drown out all ambient sounds with some additions to your workplace. A noise-canceling headphone is a good start especially if you tend to have regular meetings with coworkers and clients.

You can also add some noise-dampening devices to your room. Lining up discarded egg trays or foam along the walls, for example, can absorb a lot of noise coming from other rooms along with some thick curtains draped over your windows.

## Workout Gear

Here's the thing: it isn't healthy being seated staring at a screen for 8 hours a day. You need to do some bit of exercising to get the blood running from time to time.

Have some gear like yoga mats, stationary bicycles, and a set of dumbbells safely stored at the side that you can use during breaks. You don't your workspace to function as an elaborate gym too. You only have to make sure that you have something to do some light exercising with two to three times a day so you don't develop a sedentary lifestyle.

## Some Inspiration

Personalizing your workspace is always an option with remote work or business. However, since you are already predisposed towards that, you might as well personalize it in a manner that helps you become productive as well.

Rachael loves her home office space. She decorated it with bookshelves full of all of her favorite books, plants, her diplomas hanging on the wall, and a comfy dog bed for her lab Chester under the window. Her workspace has a large calendar with project due dates written in as well as meetings and appointments.

Pictures of your family or vacations are a good inspiration. Some quotes from famous people plastered on your wall would work here. If you have a collection of sorts, you can also place it in a way that it is always in your peripheral vision as you work.

The goal here is to give you reminders of what you are striving for. A little inspiration goes a long way in ensuring that you end every day on a high note. However, if you personalize too much, you might end up making your workspace a bit distracting for you. Just add the bare essentials to motivate your mind and nothing more.

## Building Your Skills and Toolset

When preparing all these essentials, you might be asking yourself "should I need to spend a lot to have the best possible remote work experience?" After all, those ergonomic keyboards and Wi-Fi are never going to be cheap.

The answer, honestly, is No. again, the point of earning money remotely is convenience. It is just not about physical convenience like your comfort but also about economic convenience. There is absolutely nothing in this book that will tell you to spend a lot just to have the right gear and skills.

If you are creative and resourceful, you can have everything you need without spending more than $500.00 on your equipment. As for the skills, you can learn them for free or consciously apply them to your daily habit.

And as for the inner traits to be successful, well, you can't pay to learn them. You either have them already or you don't. What this will tell you is that you must invest some effort to get what you need and have the right mentality for this kind of work/business setup. A truly successful digital nomad can create solutions that will address all their concerns and carry them through their entire career.

And with that out of the way, it's time to learn what kind of jobs are made available for you out there.

Have you noticed something odd with our discussion until now? For all our talk about earning money while being the boss of our own time, we are still doing work for someone else at their time. There's nothing boss-ish about that.

Though there is quite a lot of freedom to enjoy here, you might have noticed that a lot of remote work contracts do not provide you with a lot of control over when and how you do your work.

You are still expected to complete tasks on somebody's time using tools and methods that they approve of. The only difference is that you can do these things in the comfort of your own home.

If you are not a fan of Irony, it's time to take things a step further by making an entire enterprise of your current set of skills and tools. What that simply means is that you are now ready to enter the world of Freelance Work and Online Business.

# Chapter Two Action Steps

**Suitability:**

- Do you like to work alone?

- Are you organized? Do you have organizational daily systems?

- Can you motivate yourself to accomplish daily work?

- Are you good at prioritizing your time?

- Do you have a spot at home where you will not be distracted by a partner, kids, pets, or all the house tasks that need to be taken care of?

- Focused quiet time to concentrate on work?

- If you get off-task are you able to get yourself quickly back on task?

**Essential Remote Skills:**

- Create a daily work schedule. Is this something you can stick to as a remote worker?

  - Is there a co-worker or friend that you can check in with and that would help keep you on task? Could you do this for each other?

- Is this schedule digital or in a physical planner or both?

- Trial and error are okay until you get your best schedule figured out.

- Determine what will keep you motivated to complete projects remotely.

  - Do you have an accountability partner that you could check in with daily or weekly?

  - Could you reward yourself with (coffee? New flair pens? Every Friday afternoon off?) when you meet deadlines? What motivates you?

- Organize your workspace and work time.

  - Where are you going to complete the majority of your work?

    - Where will all your work items (printer, computer, paper, pens, planner) live?

  - Do you have all the items you need to complete your tasks for the business?

  - How can you set the tone to make this your workspace *only*?

**Do you have...**

- Communication Skills

- Teamwork

- Tech-Savviness

- Emotional Intelligence

## 3

### REMOTE WORKER, FREELANCER, OR ENTREPRENEUR?

S ebastian, an accountant in Seattle, had daydreamed about starting his own business one day, making his own hours and traveling to see his parents in Vermont whenever he wanted. During the pandemic, his company was purchased and dismantled, and one morning he opened his computer to find that email every 9-5 worker dreads: he was being laid off along with all of his co-workers.

At first, Sebastian was anxious. Although he had a bit of savings, there was a global pandemic on, who would be hiring right now? Especially, remotely, when you wouldn't have the chance to go in for a sit down for a face-to-face interview. That night, after sitting with the shock of getting laid off for the day, Sebastian got out his notebook and started writing down what his dream job (and life) looked like. He thought about whether he wanted to work in another company, be his own boss, work with one client or multiple clients, how much he would like to get paid, whether he wanted employees working for him...the list went on. The pink slip from his company gave him permission to really consider his dream and what it would take to make it work.

You picked up this book because you are interested in remote work- whether that means positioning yourself as a freelancer, contract worker, remote worker, or business owner. However, have you taken the time to really dissect what you want this life to look like? (There are some questions to get you started at the end of the chapter).

## A Brief Terms Overview

You may be familiar with the following terms, or they may be new to you. For our purposes for the rest of the book, these definitions are what I will mean for each term.

- <u>Remote Worker</u>: an employee of a business or company that works from home, either full-time or hybrid; a traditional corporate job, but from home.

  - Pros: regular hours, regular pay, solid routine, no bidding for jobs, contracted with the company, stability, 401k, health insurance

  - Cons: not much flexibility in your schedule (you need to be logged in for work when everyone else is, available for meetings, answer emails, etc.), stuck with a salary schedule, 40+ hours a week/52 weeks a year with two weeks vacation,

- Contract Worker: a short-term employee for a company; hired for a specific short-term role; contract workers will be hired for anywhere from three-twelve month stints.

  - Pros: stability and routine for longer periods of time, great pay, less applying for jobs, the potential for hire as a permanent employee (if that is something you're interested in), gain experience for freelance or entrepreneurial work,

  - Cons: have to follow company policy, required to attend meetings and may have to be available for traditional 9-5 hours depending on the contract, 40+ hour work week, no health insurance, little or no sick time or paid vacation,

- Freelance Worker: a self-employed worker no tied to any particular boss or company

  - Pros: works on only the work they are interested in, makes their own schedule, controls earning potential, different tasks/projects every week, creativity, control, can work for multiple people at the same time,

  - Cons: needs to frequently bid for jobs (daily, weekly, monthly) against other freelancers, income fluctuates, can work for multiple people at the same time, some projects may be unclear/frustrating or potential hirers will ask for additional work on top of the job description, less stability

- <u>Entrepreneur</u>: a small business owner

  - Pros: you are the boss and create the mission of the company, make your own hours, work on something you're passionate about, unlimited earning potential, you make all the decisions

  - Cons: you make all the decisions, unstable, you need to educate yourself about small business law and taxes, you need to find investors, hire/fire employees, growth of the company is dependent on how many hours you put into it, etc.

The freelance worker, contract worker, and entrepreneur who works from home- those who want to have more control over their time, career, and earning potential- is who we will be focusing on for the rest of this chapter. I am going to be using the term *Freelance*, but the concepts I go over apply to contract workers and entrepreneurs as well.

## What it means to be a Freelancer

Think of a freelancer as a less dangerous version of a mercenary soldier. Instead of being tied down to one company, you can freely move around and provide your services to anyone with the money to pay. Freelancers work when they want to work, set their own prices, and can choose to work with companies that align with their values. Freelancer Americans David and Jerry live and work in Thailand, where the cost of living is lower, and travel frequently. Freelance graphic designer Autumn only works six months out of the year (and chooses to work longer hours and six/seven days a week during those six months) then spends the rest of the year hiking, camping, and backpacking around the world.

What you need to keep in mind if you choose to go the contract, freelance, or entrepreneurial route, is that although these positions offer less stability and routine, they reward the worker with flexibility, choice, and creativity. You are the one that needs to determine what is important to you as you consider remote work, whatever that may look like.

How exactly does freelancing work, then?

Freelance jobs are essentially project-based by design. For example, you can take on an exact amount of projects every month and charge either by the complexity of the project or the hours it took to complete it. For example, say Autumn is hired to complete a business logo for a client, one that will be used on their website and on their business cards. She has an initial meeting with the client to discuss ideas and the contract. Autumn knows from previous experience that a logo project will take her 5-6 hours based on what they asked for in the design, and tells them that the project price for the logo and revision (if needed), will take X amount of time, and will be six hundred USD. If the client agrees, they all sign a contract, and the project starts.

David, writes various length blog posts and social media posts for three specific companies. These companies pay him on retainer, a certain amount per month for the blog and social media posts, but then ask for extras. The extras (a newsletter, email sequence, and web page work) are billed hourly at a rate of $125 per hour. He can decide how many extras he is willing to write a month depending on his schedule and other projects he has going.

A freelance worker has full agency; as a freelancer, you propose a deadline and set the work hours for every project. You can work on any task at any time of the day that is most convenient for you and the client would not care. So as long as you present the finished output by the set deadline, you work whenever and however is most convenient for you. That gives you a lot of flexibility and freedom to arrange your day, week, and year how you see fit. For example, if you want to drop the kids off at school and pick them up at the end of the day- no problem! Want to take a morning exercise class or have coffee with your friends? Sounds great. You set your schedule and work on your own timetable.

## Why Become a Freelancer?

Aside from being the next logical step in remote work, freelance work opens you up to enjoy several advantages which include:

- Multiple Work Opportunities – There is rarely a shortage of job postings on freelance work platforms. If you can't be hired for one, there is always another waiting on the next page.

- Control Over the Work Schedule – you can work on any task however you want and as much as you want. You don't have to work at hours when you are not at your most active and you don't need to beg for days off. In essence, you can take full advantage of when and where you are the most productive during an entire day.

- Quickly Learn New Skills – Since you will be working for different clients, you get to acquire new skills that would be otherwise hard to learn when you are bound to one employer only.

- Choose Who to Work For – If you do have a previous bad deal with one client, you can always refuse their offer and move to another. You don't have to work for someone that you don't like when you are a freelance agent.

As with everything else, going freelance does have its drawbacks. You need to consider the following disadvantages when you become a freelancer:

- Strong Need for Structure – If remote work features minimal oversight, freelance work features none at all.

You need to be highly self-motivated and committed to following your work structure to succeed here.

- Job Droughts – Especially at the start, you might have a hard time finding work.

- Constant Need to Apply – You have to regularly put yourself out in the market to earn here. It can be uncomfortable at first but you'll get used to the hiring cycle. Also, you might not need to find a job if your work is good enough. Some clients are more than willing to make a return call for future projects.

- Longer Work Hours – depending on how you plan your work, you might have to deal with more than one deadline, and you can expect to work for far longer than normal.

- No More Income Security – unlike a 9-5, your income will be sporadic at best. You might have to tighten your budget and make some adjustments until you get more clients and work under your belt.

## Becoming a Freelancer

Are you ready to dip your toes in the freelance world? Many traditional workers get their start in the freelance world while still at their company job. Do your research, brush up your resume, and start looking at job platforms.

Luckily for you, remote workers and freelancers share the same basic requirements for tools, qualities, and skills. If you've decided to become a freelance worker, there are a few more steps you need to follow to make the full transition.

## Finding a Platform, Find Your People

Sites like UpWork, Fiverr, and LinkedIn are already good places to find freelance work. Do you have Facebook, Instagram, or TikTok? Start promoting yourself, showing off work you're completing, or mention special skills you have (you would be surprised how many people are in your network already and need help with designing a webpage, writing a newsletter, or creating graphics to go with their letterhead). Make your own website on Squarespace, WordPress, etc., and start directing clients there to see your portfolio and get on your calendar. You can use social media to promote yourself and your website to potential clients.

## Build Your Profile on Freelance Platforms

Once you have registered, you will then have to establish your profile. Don't worry, there's a template that you can follow on whatever platform you register- or you can show off your creativity and do your own thing! Your platform is going to function like your resume, listing your skills, certifications, and experience as well as examples of your work!

Some platforms even have tests that you could take which will give you a rating. You can then have these ratings showcased to potential clients.

When building your profile, don't be content with just ticking some boxes. Pick and choose which skills to highlight and make a short but sweet description of yourself. Think about the work you WANT to do (instead of taking whatever falls into your lap). Of course, be mindful of your preferred rates as this determines what kind of clients you will attract.

## Never Stop Building Your Portfolio

The phrase "prove or it didn't happen" applies here. A portfolio of past jobs will tell your potential clients just what you are capable of. You can use a sample of your previous jobs (with your employer's consent, of course) or create samples for the portfolio. Pick and choose the work that best represents you.

A portfolio should showcase your talent, but it should also show a potential client WHAT IS POSSIBLE. That is why they are going to hire you after all.

## Set the Rate

Setting your rate can be a bit tricky, and beginners struggle with this, so know you're not alone. You'll get the hang of it as you immerse yourself in the freelance world and begin seeing how long a project takes you. But to start, your rate should be based on your skill set and experience. A highly experienced freelancer can command hourly or project rates by the hundreds while a beginner can set something in between a few dollars to ten.

If you have trouble determining what price to set, here's a trick: get an average of your monthly expenses and divide it by 30. If you are living on a $5,000.00 budget every month, for example, that would result in a daily rate of $160.00 to $170.00. For an hourly rate, that translates to $20.00 to $23.00 if you run an 8-hour shift. You need to also take into account that as a freelancer, you need to set aside some of your wages for taxes; they are not taken out of your compensation as they would be in a traditional job. So, using the above example, if you are making $23 an hour, you need to set aside 15-20% for taxes.

Whatever the case, do not ever work for peanuts here. Mistake beginners often make is setting their rates so low to attract potential clients. You'll be attracting clients, alright, but they would most definitely be of the exploitative and scam-y kind.

## So, what's the best way to look for a job? Here are some tips:

- Build Your Rep First – The first few projects you will get might feature comparatively low salaries. Don't get disheartened. These jobs are meant for you to build your credibility in the platform first- and even though

the pay is low, you could as the clients for good reviews to boost your reviews on the platform. These
jobs can teach you the basics of freelance work while
also allowing you to hone your skills. If you can get by
these low-paying, rep-builder jobs, you can command
better figures later on. You'll know if you have cleared
this invisible wall when you start seeing better-paying
projects on your search pages.

- Pick the Job that You are the Most Confident With –
  Remember you are also building a reputation. Pick a
  job with requirements that you can easily meet and job
  specifications that you can handle. The more capable
  you are of getting the job done, the better feedback you
  will receive. Plus, you might just impress that client
  enough to offer you another (and better-paying) project.

- Develop Your Elevator Pitch – Find a way to sell yourself in 3 sentences or less. Describe why you are the best
  person for the job and what you can bring to the table
  as far as skills and experience are concerned. It doesn't
  have to be perfect or clever. Just short enough to be
  digestible but contains all the details needed to get a
  client's attention.

It will take time for you to get higher-paying projects but you
will get there. The first few months will have you earning mod-

estly but every successful project will build on your reputation. With enough credibility, you can start commanding higher rates and have access to better-paying projects.

## Setting Up an Online Business and Becoming an Entrepreneur

Like freelancing, an online business is the next logical step in earning remotely. As a concept, online businesses work like traditional businesses in the sense that you get paid for delivering products and/or services. Shelia, a business owner, and writer, runs an online company that focuses on writing resumes/CVs, cover letters, networking classes, and how to position yourself on LinkedIn or recruiters to be hired. Meghan is a health coach for moms, publishes a podcast, and created a workbook. Devin runs a financial consulting business that shows other businesses how to cut costs and maximize profits. And Ashley runs her own graphic design business and is booked through the next year.

As an online business owner, you don't need to deal with the usual hurdles of setting up a traditional, brick-and-mortar business like incorporation and finding capital.

So, what do you need for your online business? This might surprise you but you already have most of what you need to get it started. For starters, you have a working computer and access to the internet. You'll probably need to set up a basic website that at least allows potential clients to read about you, see your work, and contact you. Everything else depends on what you need to deliver your services and get paid for them.

As for advantages, the same perks with freelance work will apply. You don't need an office to run your business and there's no definite set of work hours. Your business exists so as long as you have your computer, are awake, and can render whatever you are offering to your clients. (A word of caution here- new business owners often have to work over and above 40 hours a week to get the ball rolling. You need to consider if this is the right season and if you have enough time to devote to starting a business.)

That being said, the earning potential here is quite high even when compared to freelance work. So as long as you have the means to meet the demands of your clientele, you can earn as much as 5 figures every week.

Of course, this setup is rather demanding. You will need to consider a few things as well before you even think about setting up your own remote online business.

## Your Business plan

As you will be starting this business by yourself, there is no need to follow a definite format. Your business plan is essentially a statement declaring what you want to do and how you will go about doing it.

Start by determining what kind of business you want to offer. Will you be offering a service (like resume writing or design) or a product (like jewlery or a course). Aside from that, you want to establish what you want to achieve. Financial independence, for example, is already a good goal. But you might make it specific by adding in a particular figure. This way, you have some tangible goal to focus all your efforts on.

## Your Business Model

Even if your business has no physical makeup, you should at least establish how it operates. From the organizational chart to the delivery of your products and services and even the cash flow, everything that could be relevant to the operation of your business must be set on paper. (There are many good examples available online).

Also, you should always consider the future. What exactly will your business look like if it succeeds in the first few years? What will be its clientele? Will you need to put up a website later on? How much will it earn? Will you need to hire others and when will you do that? If you expand your offerings, are you okay with your company growing or do you want to remain small? These are just some of the things that you must establish at this point.

Again, you are free to define your business model as you please. However, there is one quality that your online business model must possess. It must, at some point, in time, set you up for legitimacy.

Simply put, your model as defined should allow for the brand to grow into a bona fide company. This means that it should be open for the opportunity to hire more people aside from you, establish relationships with a broader client base, and earn money for all employees and investors.

## Online Business Ideas

Everything can sound a bit overwhelming right now. The question that you would like to ask is this:

Where do I start?

There are quite a lot of business opportunities out there- so, so many! However, to give you some inspiration, here are some of the online business ideas that net a healthy amount of profit.

## Blogging and Social Networking

The algorithm updates in the last few years have pushed for more actionable and personable information in the results pages. This means that content like blog posts and social media posts are getting more traction now than conventional articles and list-type content.

This content can draw in a considerable audience. The way to monetize these pages is by signing up for affiliate marketing programs and pay-per-click advertisements.

And there are companies out there that are willing enough to pay blogs and social media handles to provide content for their products. The more following these handles get, the larger the income potential will be.

On an individual basis, the income is barely enough to even register as earnings. However, pages that draw in crowds by the millions combined with strong social interactions can result in income up to the thousands every week.

## Being a Social Influencer

Similar to blogging, social influencing works on the premise of income through attention. How it works is quite simple: an influencer recommends something like a brand to their followers. These followers, in turn, consume whatever product the brand has to offer.

This type of promotional service is not something that you can do right away, however. First, you need Clout and that involves quite a lot of non-promotional work to build your audience.

In other words, you need to have some form of Personality to gain a following. Invest in your social media handles and make sure that you are not camera-shy. Spend some time doing whatever is interesting like playing a videogame or traveling.

In time, and if you have the charisma, you will start to gain a following. And in time, you can start leveraging your influence on companies that need to reach out organically to established audiences.

## Software Development

This remote business idea particularly pays well if you know how to code. The demand for software-based products is quite high right now and clients are looking for someone who can translate their concepts into functional software.

Aside from that, being a remote software developer has the highest potential to grow into a larger, legitimate company. You might be taking in the few odd programming jobs in your first months but would eventually start pitching your software later on.

## Responsive Website Design

It's easy to think that site design is no longer in demand since tools like WordPress has made the process more accommodating for people with zero coding skills. However, there is stronger demand nowadays for responsive website design.

Responsive site design is simply a webpage's ability to adjust to any browser size and device navigation system. Designing websites to be responsive from the ground up is something that not a lot of people are capable of performing.

What's even more surprising is you don't have to spend a lot as far as tools are concerned to get started here. Something as simple as Notepad is good enough to write code in. You can opt for more elaborate setups once your business has thrived.

# eBooks and Content Writing

Writing content for clients has always had decent income potential. However, it takes a while for you to earn a great deal of money per project here.

If you ever had any idea to share with the world, make a book out of it. There are platforms out there like Amazon where you can sell your eBooks for a reasonable fee.

As for how much you should charge for every download of your book, the rule of thumb is that the price should scale with the level of difficulty of the subject matter. The more technical the subjects that a book will cover, the more expensive it should be to download.

If long-form content is not your style, you can also partner with marketing companies that want people to create "copy" (that's a marketing term for informative yet advertiseable content) for them.

The best part of this business model is that you don't need anything else to start it. All you need is a recent copy of Microsoft Word or any similar document editor and you're good to go.

# Website Flipping

This business model takes a leaf from real estate with its concept. Simply put, you buy websites, invest in improving them, and then sell them to the market for a higher price.

There are a lot of domain names out there that are in high demand. If you can buy them cheap, you can have them sold at a more expensive price at a later time.

That being said, this business idea works best if you exactly know what you are doing. You can't just buy all the domain names. You have to be strategic with your purchases. Also, you have to have a strong background in website infrastructure to make your websites attractive to potential buyers.

## SEO and SMO Consulting

If you have done work for internet marketing firms and have done some site design by the side, you could use those skills to audit the internet presence of companies and individuals. The end goal, of course, is to make their pages rank higher in the search engine results pages.

Again, what makes this business model attractive is that you are already using the skills and tools that you have already honed as a remote worker. Of course, consultancy is not just about telling brands what to do. You might even create content your-self to present as proof of concept to your clients.

The only drawback here is that you have to build on your credibility first to get clients. You can present samples of your previous work to show that you know what you are doing, however.

Also, this kind of field is notorious for constant updates. You have to regularly learn new things just to keep up with changing standards.

# Teaching

Let's assume that you have something interesting to share with the rest of the world. Instead of turning it into book form, you can directly express your thoughts through an online learning platform.

Sites like uDemy can host virtual learning courses prepared by yourself where you teach people topics that you are an expert at. You will get paid for every student that enrolls in your courses.

What makes this business idea neat is that you can plan your content. You don't have to teach everything to your students in one sitting. You can stretch the course into several modules and programs to maximize profit.

Also, the content you produce is "evergreen". This means that every piece of information you share will remain actionable so as long as they are relevant. Your courses will continue to earn you money so as long as they are made available on the learning platforms.

# Still Stumped?

Start with what you know best. You know yourself better than anyone. What are you good at?

If you are the most organized of your friends (for example, when you all travel to Cancun for vacation, you're the one who finds the best flight deals, hotel deals, plans the itinerary with a binder and colored tabs for each section) could you do something with organization or travel? What if you offered an organizational service to other business or corporate leaders? Or maybe you love arranging music. What if you offered to design the intro and outro music for new podcast launches?

Your time spent doing remote jobs (or even traditional jobs) should have equipped you with the skills and knowledge to complete tasks. These are assets themselves that you can share with others. If you have something interesting and actionable to offer to the market, chances are that people will pay top dollar for it.

Remember, how you attract clients either as a freelancer or as an online business owner is a matter of PRESENTATION. So as long as people find value in what you have to say or offer, then you can monetize your skills and experience.

## Time Management as a Freelancer and/or Business Owner

So, we will cover this in more depth in a following chapter on productivity.

Will you have to juggle multiple jobs or projects as a freelancer or business owner? In the beginning, yes. Some freelancers en-joy having multiple jobs going at the same time, as it provides variety. Other freelancers find it stressful. You will have to find what works for you. Business owners will have to wear various hats (receptionist, accountant, content creator, etc.) when they are first starting out. As I mentioned before, when you initially start working in the freelance/entrepreneur world, you will have to work more at the start).

But, to think about this question on a deeper level, let's divide a particular day into three sections. One section is for work, another for attending to personal matters, and another for rest. It does not matter if all sections are not equal in length. What matters is that every single person is given these 3 sections per day.

Each section will affect our physical and mental energies. The work section takes the most out of it. The personal concerns section can also take a considerable portion depending on family obligations (giving time to a partner, aging parents, and children, exercise, cleaning, cooking, hobbies, etc.). Finally, the rest section allows us to replenish these energies back to optimal levels.

By having multiple jobs, you also increase the period for your work section.

In the long term, you run the risk of burning yourself out and losing motivation. There are ways to mitigate the effects but just know that you can only do so much at any given time of the day. It is paramount that you create a freelance routine and optimize the time you are working.

## Organization and Consistency

It bears repeating that the key to success here is not increasing the strain but optimizing the effort. That might require you to lengthen your work so that the usual overtime becomes regular work time. However, it should not be too long to render you in a condition requiring visits to the local clinic (or therapist!).

Think of it like that circus trick where the clown has to juggle multiple things at once. You are most likely to successfully manage this fine balance if you do not panic. Here's how:

## Preparation

Now, if your first job is already covering 35 to 40 hours of that combined 60 hours, then you do have not much for a full-time second or third job. In some cases, you are better off not having a second job for now.

- Determine Availability – Identify when and how available you will be for your other jobs. This is why you should pick jobs that are not that strict when it comes to requiring synchronized work. This allows you to pick the most convenient time for you to perform tasks there.

  And what about meetings? Just remember when that day is set and make sure that you are available. And if not, give a very plausible reason why. But if attendance is mandatory, you have no choice but to make amendments. This is why picking jobs with flexible schedules are necessary.

- Never Sacrifice Your Joys – Do not ever take time out from the activities that help you relax. Things like hobbies, leisure time, and even sleeping time should not be sacrificed so you could be productive for multiple employers. These activities are one of your several outlets to avoid burnout.

- Make a schedule – Mark the hours of the day when you are preoccupied with your first job. This will give you a realistic view of how much you can devote your time to your new work. It might also help in negotiating work hours for your other employer.

## Follow a Routine

- Your only route to success here lies in following a plan to the letter. Your ability to commit to a schedule is what will make you effective as a remote worker. But when you have more than one job, being able to stick to a schedule becomes more than necessary.

- If possible, plan the entire work week. Consider when you will start working for one job and then for the other. Also, do take into consideration any other extra tasks that might pop up or emergency appointments. Speak with your employers about the scheduling of these tasks and make sure that they don't clash.

• And if you are the type that needs to be thoroughly reminded, use your to-do apps to organize your tasks and set up reminders. And while we are talking about your schedule....

## Remember to Attend to Personal Matters, Too

• You always run the risk of losing time for the other areas of your life if you work more than one job a day. If you are not careful, you could end a day with the laundry left unwashed, a pile of dirty dishes at the sink, an empty cupboard, and a dusty house. You might even forget if you have taken a bath for that day.

• Again, taking care of yourself should not be sacrificed just so you could be doubly productive. You don't even need 3 hours to do everything necessary for your well-being. Save time by getting all that you need from the grocery for a week.

• As for cleaning, you can either do it before you start your work or after. The point is that you should include all the activities necessary for your well-being as part of your schedule, too. Once included, all that is left to do is for you to stick to the plan.

## Remember To Socialize, Too

- This tip is something that should be obvious to you. Your goal for remote work is to have more time to spend with those that you love. And even if you have more than one job now, you should still be able to meet your friends and family.

- It's often tempting to sacrifice your time to meet deadlines. After all, you think you could meet them once you have cleared up your schedule.

- So your next best solution here is to give yourself a specific day where you can socialize. Friday nights or the weekends are great options. The point is that you also need to recharge yourself by interacting with other people.

# Chapter Three Action Steps

**Answer the following questions to get a better idea about what type of remote worker you want to be...**

- What would your **<u>dream</u>** remote job be?

  - How can you make this happen?

- Would you like the stability of working remotely (at home) but employed by a company as a 9-5 employee?

- Do you want to make your own schedule?

- Do you want to make and maintain your own website for clients to see your work and connect with you?

- Would you prefer a compromise between a traditional worker at a 9-5 job and a freelance worker- working on 3-6-9 month contracts for large companies?

- Do you have letters of reference and/or a portfolio set up for bosses/clients?

- Are you prepared to bid for jobs as a freelancer (daily, weekly, or monthly)?

- Are you familiar with sites like Upwork, LinkedIn, and Fivver?

- Could you handle making more income some months and less income other months?

- Do you want to be in charge of your earning potential?

- Would you like to have people work for you? (other people in the same business, virtual assistants, or branch out)?

    ○ If you were the boss, what would this look like?

    ○ What do you think it takes to run a business?

# 4

— · —

## GETTING HIRED

M arcy began freelance writing during the pandemic. Her 9-5 job cut her hours in half, and she found that she had the time to start building a business that she always dreamed about. She watched YouTube videos on freelance writing and marketing, put together a rudimentary website, created a few pieces for her portfolio, and started messaging friends as leads...and nothing happened. So, Marcy started looking at jobs on Upwork and created a LinkedIn profile.

After a couple of weeks, a recruiter who had multiple open jobs contacted her, telling her that she was "a perfect fit" and "they were willing to double her current asking price" for jobs. Marcy signed on, paying a fee to work with the recruiting company (she was told it would help promote her work on their site). She never heard from the recruiting company again.

Sound familiar? Have you heard horror stories like this on social media?

Learning what you can apply for in the remote job market is the first hurdle. Next, we will find a job that matches your skills and preferences. But just like any traditional job search, looking for a remote job does have its challenges. It is not only about giving the impression that you are the best person for the job; it is also about showing that you are the best freelancer for the job.

## Learning the Language

First things first, you have to understand that not all companies have the same definition of what constitutes "remote or free-lance work". So, what do companies mean when they say that your job is a "remote" type? Here are some examples:

- Fully Remote – When a company says this, what they mean is that every one of their employees is required to work remotely. This is ideal for you as it fits what you already know about remote work. It would also mean that everyone is on the same page when it comes to complying with work guidelines.

- Online Job – The job that you are applying for can only be done online or through a virtual workplace. This also means that the employer is assuming that you have all the essentials to carry out online work properly sorted out.

- Work-From-Anywhere – A job with this arrangement will have no geographical limits. Does it mean that it is remote? In most cases, yes. Will it be fully virtual? In some cases, the answer is no.

- Hybrid – The employer requires you to be as flexible as possible with your work. You might be remotely working for a few months and then shift to face-to-face work, depending on new guidelines.

Note: Why learn the terminologies used by employers? Because the work agreement you might sign up for will be different from what you were expecting. For example, you might be expecting a fully remote setup but the agreement implies an agile work setup. That means you might be remote for one time and then have to show up at an office later.

What this requires from you is to be careful with whatever job post you are replying to. Take the time to understand what they mean when it comes to their remote job offer. This way, you don't sign yourself up for a job that will put you at a disadvantage.

So what does it mean when we say that not all remote jobs are equal? As the discussion above will tell you, they don't have the same description or requirements. You might be surprised that some "remote" jobs are actually "hybrid jobs". These jobs allow you to do your tasks remotely but might require you to show up at an office from time to time. Troy, a marketer, and Joyce, a public relations employee for a large bank, both work in the hybrid structure. They like working from home and also going into work two days a week for collaboration and connection with their team.

There will also be some remote jobs that have a location restriction. Unless you can relocate to a new place, you should apply for these jobs only if you are within the same region, state, province, or country. You may have a friend that is always posting pictures of themselves with a computer at the beach. While that sounds nice, it is the exception. The majority of online jobs will require you to have a stable internet connection at the very least. Many will ask you to be in a certain region or country.

Your best solution in this part is to always read the job description before applying.

## Watching Out for Scams

"Make a million dollars working only one hour a day...," "If you can do basic addition, we're looking for you- work as much or as little as you want and make thousands..." You've heard this all your life- if it sounds too good to be true, it is too good to be true. The remote jobs market has attracted the attention of a lot of scammers. So how do you avoid them? Luckily, if you know what to look for, you won't waste your time on scams.

First, you have to know the red flags which include the following:

## Too Good to be True Offers

In most cases, you have to trust what your intuition is telling you. Offers like unlimited earning potential, a lot of perks for an entry-level position, and low qualifications for high-paying positions are tell-tale signs that you might be led into a potential scam.

## Not a Lot of Company Information

Normally, companies should have a considerable presence on-line. This way, job seekers could learn everything about them before they even consider applying. A major red flag to watch out for if you can't find anything worth reading about the company. From reviews to web pages and even a social media account. If you can't find any information about them, this might be a scam. If they do have a web page, but when you go to the web page there is only the landing page with no other linked pages (like "About Us," "Company History," "Departments," and "Employment Opportunities" for example), that is a red flag.

In line with this, be mindful of the ages of their content. If their web pages, social media handles, and other pages are made within a week or a month with no one to vouch for them, you should approach the company with caution.

## Bot Reviews

Check the quality of their followers. Most scams pay for bots to boost up their profiles on sites like LinkedIn and other business review sites.

How would you know that you are reading the review of bots? Check if they say the same thing over and over, format, term usage, misspellings, and all. Also, check how many reviews these bots have given. If it is only for that company, you should be worried.

## An Overly Eager Recruiter

One telltale sign of a scam is if the recruiter or employer is all too eager to get you started and promises you the moon and the stars. Naturally, it usually takes companies several weeks to months before your application is approved and you start working. What would be odd, however, is if you start working immediately after an interview.

A legitimate employer weighs its decisions thoroughly by screening all applicants. Also, they would rather let you be comfortable as possible and not pressure you to start working for them.

## Paying for Work or to Find You a Job

In the olden days, this was called a "placement fee". A scammer will come up with a handful of reasons why you need to pay before you can start working. Here's the thing, though: they're the ones that are supposed to pay you. It makes absolutely no sense to pay a company so you could earn money from them.

A recent example from Upwork comes to mind. The scammers would post a job (which was too good to be true), complete a pretend interview over messaging/email, and then "hire" the applicants. The scammers would then ask the hire to pay them five hundred dollars as an "equipment" charge, claiming the charge would be fully reimbursed once the hire received the promised equipment (a computer, printer, and phone). The hire would send in the five hundred dollars and never hear from the scammers again. (Yes, this happened.)

That being said, there's a difference between paying for your work and paying a subscription fee for a legitimate remote job board. Just keep that in mind when looking for remote work.

## Poor Communication Skills

This is one of the easiest red flags to notice. A legitimate company hires a professional to proofread its work before sending it out to someone. So, if their communications are full of spelling and grammatical errors, you'll know it's a scam.

There is also a recent trend where scammers over-correct themselves and use fancy words or phrases when talking to you. This is easier to spot because it's common sense to talk to someone in plain and simple English for an easy exchange of ideas.

## What Scams should you be on the lookout for?

## 1. The Faulty Check

How this works is quite ingenious, to be honest. The company sends you a check with an amount that is way more than your agreed salary. You tell them that their payment is a bit too much than what was agreed. They then tell you that they made an honest mistake and instruct you to send the difference.

When you send the difference back, the trap is sprung. You then try to cash out their check and find out that it bounced. The scammer stops talking to you and they have made off with a handful of your money.

## 2. Recruit-to-Earn

Just a bit of clarification here: not all Multi-Level Marketing schemes are scams. However, a lot of scammers use this scheme to make money for you in a semi-legitimate way.

This scheme works well in remote sales jobs as it requires you to buy the products you will be selling. Now, the company will employ this pyramid scheme where you get to earn from every person you recruited personally. At the same time, you get to earn from every person that your recruit recruited otherwise known as a "down line".

Although you might be earning, it is the people at the very top of this pyramid that earn the most. This is because everyone else down the line has to pay for the products that they are going to sell. It's a lot of complicated work for money that you could otherwise earn regularly from a legitimate entry-level job.

## 3. The Re-Ship

This is a fairly dangerous scam as every victim is also an accomplice to a crime. This work-at-home type of job have you repackaging "orders" to be sent to other stations across the country.

The only problem is that most of the items you are re-shipping are most likely stolen from legitimate orders. Scammers hire re-shippers as they make for perfect proxies in case the entire operation is discovered. These re-shippers get criminally charged while the masterminds relocate and do the scam somewhere else.

*Important Reminder*

These are just some of the ways that you can get scammed while looking for a remote job. In some cases, you might even fall for a completely legitimate-looking scam with none of the red flags showing up.

## Where to Look

Now that you know what to look for in a remote job, the next challenge is to find out where these jobs are posted. A lot of job boards on the Internet do focus on all types of remote work. Here's a tip, however: if you want to find the job that suits you, look for a job board that specializes in a certain job or field.

You can also broaden your search by tapping into people that are already working remotely. Ask them how they found their job as well as some tips for applying. If you are lucky, their company might be on the lookout for an applicant that fits your description.

Also, be mindful of the language used in these job posts. Any post that mentions "work-life balance" and "flexibility" would imply that these jobs are remote by design. But just to be safe, just read through all the details. The requirements would also tell you if a job is remote especially if they require an internet connection and a working computer.

## The Right Job Type

Like every job in the conventional job market, remote jobs can come on a full-time, part-time, freelance, or contractual basis. The most work-from-home friendly job types are usually freelancing and contract positions since they offer the most flexibility in terms of hours and working days.

However, there are some full-time and part-time remote jobs that offer a high degree of flexibility as well. It all depends on the employer and the specific job requirements. When searching for a remote job, be sure to specify your desired job type in your search criteria to ensure that you only see relevant results.

## How to Sell Yourself

So, how do you sell your skills? First, you have to mention your job experience. Make sure to directly mention what companies you previously worked for and for how long. If this isn't your first try at remote work, also make sure to mention what kind of remote jobs you have worked for, for what company, and for how long.

But what if you don't have any previous remote work experience? It all comes down to how you present information. You might have to do some research as well to find which of your previous experiences can make you qualified for a remote job.

Start with your previous co-workers and clients. Were they located in a different place? Have you coordinated meetings with them despite the different timelines? Did you collaborate on a successful project? What about the tools, skills, and software you use to complete these projects? Take the time to highlight your successes in these areas.

Even if you have never done any remote job, remember that many of the skills you have developed in your previous work will make you successful as a remote worker. Employers want remote work applicants that can display the following skills:

- Self-motivation

- Focus

- Adaptability to technology

- Time management

- Strong communication skills

Think about how you managed to display these skills before. Were you ever given projects that you managed to complete on time with minimal oversight from your superiors? Then, you got time management and self-motivation. Was there a project that required you to learn new software? That would mean that you are comfortable with changing technology. And so on.

The goal here is to always sell yourself with the skills you have attained. That would require some serious self-inventory and good presentation skills on your part. You might be surprised at just how many of the skills you have already perfected make you a qualified applicant for any remote job you are applying for.

## The Interview

In a sense, an interview for a remote job shares the same elements as a face-to-face interview. The only difference is that you and the interviewer are not conversing in the same room.

So, how you approach an interview for your remote job should be treated with the same degree of care and preparation as your regular job interview. That being said, there are a few special steps to remember.

## Preparation

Remote job interviews tend to be done over the phone or through a video chat. At this part, you can already show your understanding of technology by getting the basics right.

Mind your setup which will serve as the background for the interview. Make sure that everything is tidy and professional-looking. Also, make sure that there will be no interruptions during the interview.

Some noise cancellers can work here. Telling everybody else living with you that you're going to have an interview will be important. Either way, just make sure that the interview has your undivided attention for half an hour or so.

Third, make sure that everything is in working order before the interview. The last thing you would want to do is to make the interviewer wait while you set something up. That also gives the impression that you are not as tech-savvy as you would want to appear.

## Answering Questions

No matter how conversational things get, interviewers always follow a particular flow when conducting their interviews. Following the STAR method of answering questions can be a great way to make sure you are providing the interviewer with the most complete and concise answers possible.

The **STAR method** is an acronym that stands for **situation, task, action**, and **result**. Answering questions using this method can help you provide well-rounded answers that show off your problem-solving skills and ability to think on your feet.

When answering questions using the STAR method, first take a moment to describe the situation you were in when the task at hand was assigned to you. Then, describe the task itself and what your specific goals were. After that, detail the actions you took to complete the task, and finally, describe the results of your efforts.

Using the STAR method can help ensure that your answers are both complete and concise, two qualities that all great interviewers are looking for. So next time you're in an interview, try using the STAR method to answer questions and see how it can help you ace the interview!

# Mind Your Verbal and Non-Verbal Cues

Your language in an interview goes beyond the level of complexity that you use. It will also involve the terms that you usually inject to maintain your trail of thought.

If possible, avoid using filler words like "Uhm", "er", "ah", "you know", "literally", "like," "actually", and "okay". This gives the impression that you are trying to scramble for an answer that you are not sure about.

Your word usage also determines how confident you are with your answers. If possible, do not say "I think" or "maybe" unless you are asked for an opinion. When the question is quite subjective by design i.e. something with a definite answer, say "I believe" or "As far as I am concerned". These phrases embody a more authoritative and confident stature without coming off as intimidating or arrogant.

Interviewers are also quite keen on what you are not saying to them verbally. Your body, for instance, can give off a lot of signs that it is not comfortable when being interrogated and it clearly shows during an interview.

What you should aim for is a relaxed and composed body structure. Try to practice looking yourself in the eye in the mirror for a few days. Interviewers are quite keen on eye contact. (Just remember to blink once in a while so you don't creepy).

Next would be your arms. Do not ever cross them in an interview as they give the impression that you are defensive or hostile. If you are a person with a tendency towards fidgeting or any exaggerated hand movement, try clasping your hands and keep them in throughout the interview.

And if you can't avoid doing any of those, keep your hands on your lap and try positioning your camera so that only the forearms above could be seen. The advantage of virtual interviews is that interviewees do not mind if they can't have a full-screen view of their upper body.

The goal here is to appear calm and confident when talking to another person. The interview is your opportunity to showcase your ability to convey information in a format that is easy to understand and maintain a conversation with.

## Remember: Presentation Matters

Looking for a remote job is not that hard as compared to a regular job. However, that won't mean to say that you should not put in the necessary effort to get the best prospects.

Always remember that much of what gets you through any job application is Presentation. From your skills to your achievements and even the format of your resume, how you put yourself out for employers will still matter in the remote job market.

And if you do land a job, congratulations! Once you do get the hang of your current job, you might want to consider taking things to the next level.....

Congratulations, You're Hired!

# How to Transition to a Remote Work Environment

The success of work-from-home setup in various lines of business and company types has led to an increase in its popularity. From customer care to web developers, the transfer of worksites from towering skyscraper buildings to the comfort of our homes has proven efficient. In studies conducted by the likes of Forbes, Gallup, and FlexJobs, it has been shown that employees who work remotely are not only more productive but also have lower stress levels. These reasons alone led to reviews of company policies on functions and workspace of their employees. In addition to these, companies may benefit from cost savings in terms of office rental and maintenance, employee attrition, and the increased likelihood of a larger talent pool to choose from when hiring.

# Change is Inevitable

This rising system in the corporate world has caused various changes for employees, employers, and companies themselves. The most significant of which is having to adjust to working in a remote environment.

Some may find it way too abrupt. Some may look at it late. Working from home isn't new especially to people who have been in freelance or contract-based work for a long time. The recent events have, however, forced full-time employees in various companies to comply with the arrangement almost instantaneously.

## Boost Our Connectivity and Integrity

The work-from-home setup is also a trust exercise between employer and employee. With no one physically looking over your shoulder, it is essential, to be honest, and open communication with your team or supervisor. Ascertain that you have understood the setup, the expectations, and the deadlines of your work.

Set a schedule and agree on deadlines. This will give you a sense of structure and avoid the feeling of being all over the place. Remember that most businesses run on capital and time. Wasting either one will not only hurt the company but may also get you into trouble. Aside from setting a schedule, it is important to set boundaries as well. Let your team or supervisor know what hours you are available and when you are not. This way, they won't be expecting quick turnaround times on tasks outside of work hours.

Keep the communication lines open at all times. If we need help or clarification on something, do not hesitate to reach out. We may also consider using applications that will help us keep track of our work progress or help us communicate with our team more efficiently.

Easing into a remote work environment may be a bit challenging at first, but it is doable with the right mindset and preparation. Just remember to have a dedicated workspace, the necessary tools, and good connectivity. Be honest and open with your employer. The same goes for your team or supervisor. They should also feel free to contact you whenever they need to.

Assuming that you have a dedicated workspace and the basic tools you need, the next thing you need to do is boost your connectivity and integrity.

## Rewire: Adjusting to New Routine

Setting a new routine won't easy as pie. It will take some time to get used to not having to commute every day and being in the same room as our colleagues. The key is to be patient and give yourself time to adapt. The first few days or weeks may be a bit rocky as we try to find our footing. During this time, it is important to be understanding and easy on ourselves. Just like anything else, the more we do it, the easier it gets.

Create a daily or weekly routine and stick to it as much as possible. This will help our bodies and minds adjust to the new normal. Try to get up at the same time every day and create a dedicated workspace. If we can, avoid working in bed or on the couch.

Start our day with easy tasks to help us ease into work mode. Once we're done with the easier stuff, move on to more challenging tasks. This will help you avoid feeling overwhelmed by your workload and increase your sense of accomplishment as the day goes by.

Keeping a list of things to do will also help us stay on track and avoid forgetting important tasks. This can be in the form of a daily or weekly to-do list. Place your accomplishment tracklist on a visible spot to help keep you motivated. Checking things off our list as we complete them will give us a sense of satisfaction and progress.

Dressing up for work may boost our productivity. It doesn't have to be anything too fancy. Just put on something that makes you feel good and ready to conquer the day.

## Boss Up Against Distractions

A home is a place of safety and comfort, yes. But work is work, and we need to be able to focus on the tasks at hand. It is important to establish rules with ourselves and others in our household to help minimize distractions. If you live with others, it is important to set some ground rules. Ensure the separation of work and familial duties during work hours. This can be a difficult feat, especially for parents. But it is important to set some boundaries. If possible, hire a babysitter or ask a family member to watch the kids for a couple of hours so you can focus on work. Let them know when you are working and shouldn't be disturbed unless it's an emergency.

That also means no more TV, social media, or any other form of entertainment that can take your focus away from work. You need to be in a place where you can focus on your work and nothing else. The temptation to sit comfortably in front of your favorite Netflix series or scroll through social media can be strong. But if you want to be productive, you need to find the willpower to resist these temptations.

In case background noise is a problem, consider investing in a good pair of noise-canceling headphones. This will help you focus on your work and tune out any distractions. We may not be able to control everything, but we can certainly try our best to create a conducive environment for work.

## Time is a Friend

No one should expect the shift of work to be easy. Not you, not the bosses, nor the company policymakers. It is a big change that will take some time for us to get used to. The key is to be patient and give ourselves time to adjust. Expect several frustrations along the way as we try to find our grip in the process of transition. Anticipate a few hitches and roadblocks, but do not be discouraged. The more we try, the easier it will become eventually. Time is a friend for all who undergo this shift.

Another important thing to remember is that we are not alone in this transition. Many others are going through the same thing. Accept support and understanding from your loved ones. Do not hesitate to reach out to your friends, family, or colleagues. With all these, one thing is for sure, the success of the transition to a remote work environment is a win-win situation for both the company and the employees.

# Chapter Four Action Steps

- Brainstorm your skills for your freelance resume and interviews

- Get references from past employers and co-workers

  - If possible, ask for them to mention your organization, time management, ability to work under a schedule and meet deadlines, response to feedback, and self-motivation

- Put together a portfolio of your best work

- Join LinkedIn and start checking out the platform in order to get comfortable with it

- Start looking for other platforms where you can find your preferred freelance work (like writing, designing, organization skills, etc.)

- Join networking opportunities for freelancers and small business owners

- Get freelancing, small business, and entrepreneur books from the library.

# 5

## THE PILLARS OF PRODUCTIVITY

Have you ever tried to complete a project while also homeschooling your kids, doing laundry, potty training a puppy, and answering co-workers' emails? Which of these deserves the most attention? Are you completing all of these with focus and to the best of your ability? Or, like me, are you wondering what is falling through the cracks as you type a quick email on your phone while answering your son's math question?

We all think that we're amazing multitaskers (really, we do- studies show that we believe this), but the truth is that the human brain is literally unable to multitask well. Now, we can either focus on one task and do a great job or juggle multiple things at the same time and do a mediocre job- but we CANNOT do both.

So, is multitasking good for productivity?

## The Concept of Productivity

At the risk of sounding cliché, your ability to be productive lies on your mind. To be productive, you have to understand how the brain works.

The human brain deals with two classes of actions. The first set is the ones that have been committed to instinct, muscle memory, and reflexes. These actions require less mental energy as the brain puts them on a short list of things to do every hour or second. Some of the actions included in this set are breathing, muscle coordination, balancing while standing or walking, and other basic functions.

However, there is a second set of actions that are too complex or deliberate to be committed to mere muscle memory. Some of these actions include completing a document, learning something new, cooking, preparing an income tax report, fixing the fence, etc. For these deliberate actions, the brain is required to do one thing: **focus**. The ability to concentrate is important in complex actions. The more focused the mind is, the more likely it is to succeed in finishing a task.

Can the brain maintain this focused state for long periods of time? The short answer is no. It's not designed that way. This state of hyper-focus can make us lose track of everything else happening around us which is equally problematic. This is why the brain needs to snap out of it once in a while.

Aside from that, focusing expends our finite mental energies. Every person has a set amount of this energy every day. We drain most of our mental focus during work, especially complicated, intricate, skilled, or new work, which is why we are left physically exhausted in the evening. Do you ever wonder why all you want to do in the evening is crash on the couch and rewatch your favorite Hulu show? It's because your brain is tired.

The point is that achieving the hyper-focused state is crucial to being productive, but it can only be sustained for so long. Much of your attempts to become more productive will involve trying to induce this state in yourself and taking advantage of it.

## Duration

How long can anyone stay hyper-focused? There is no definite answer to this; everyone is different, just like everyone can engage in different amounts of physical activity based on their health and condition. However, experts state that a normal brain can maintain this state for somewhere between 30 minutes to 78 minutes. This period does not account for distractions and other impulses that the brain might pick up.

It does give us a reasonable time frame as to how long can our brain concentrate on something before it needs a break. Once the brain has relaxed, it can then be induced into this hyper-focused state once more. And, just like bodybuilders can build muscle, you can build upon your brain's ability to maintain focus.

So, the strategy of becoming productive is maintaining this sequence of focusing, breaking, and focusing again throughout the entire day.

## Increasing Productivity

Since productivity is an issue of Mind over Matter, much of what you can do to become productive at home is to change your perspective. There are several strategies to do this which include the following:

## Be a "Morning" Person

Does this mean that you have to become someone who is already active way before sunrise? Not really. Remember that every person has a work schedule. You might be someone who loves working at night or someone who is at their most active during noon.

What this means, however, is that you should have developed a routine that gets your brain fired up at your "morning" i.e. that time of the day when you rise from your long sleep. One other benefit of a "morning" routine is that it helps you take control of your time by adding structure to your day the very second it starts.

What should your routine be, then? There is no definite answer here as each person has their way of adding structure to their life.

Does this involve 30 minutes of YouTube videos or reading? Does it involve 2 or 3 rounds of your favorite videogame to get pumped up? Does it involve a healthy breakfast regardless of the time and having a yoga session? By all means, have those included in your routine! Your goal here is to make yourself as upbeat and energetic as possible so you could begin work immediately.

## Three Workplace Productivity Pillars

The one element that is crucial to your productivity remains Structure. A sense of structure is what gives consistency to your output and stability to your work pace. To establish that structure, you must base all your efforts on three pillars.

## Baby Steps

There is no such thing as overnight perfection. Nothing sustainable was ever applied immediately and without error.

If you have some trouble adjusting to productivity at home, it is a better idea to allow change to occur piece by piece. This helps the mind ease into a new regime one step after another. For instance, if a content writer cannot produce 5 500-word articles every day, then they could settle for 3. And once they get the hang of that standard, they then can move to 4 and then 5.

You will find out that making the new components compatible with what you already have is a more effective way of embracing productivity as opposed to shocking the entire system with massive, sweeping changes.

## Accountability

It is easy to blame everything else as to why you can't be productive where you are. You can say that the workload is too heavy or that your equipment is poor or that there are just too many things to distract you at home. And so on.

Remember that the one thing that can truly hold you back from doing more than what you are comfortable with is you. Productivity, after all, is a state of mind which means that you have way more control over what you expose yourself to than you think.

So, in practice, it is not that you can switch tabs to Facebook or Youtube that makes you unproductive. You are entertaining the thought of changing tabs, that matters more. It is not that your neighbors or family members are noisy. It is that you never even attempted to soundproof your workplace, to begin with.

In all things, be it success or failure, the buck should stop with you.

## Self-Compassion

Becoming overly critical of yourself and your output is a pitfall you should try to avoid as a remote worker. This is because there is always that tendency to overcorrect. And when you overcorrect, you sacrifice a bit of your well-being just to reach deadlines.

Remember that you are not perfect. This means only that you are bound to make some mistakes. There might even be days when you cannot finish your tasks because of a factor that you failed to anticipate.

And if you do fail to meet your daily quota, you should avoid criticizing yourself too much. Instead, focus on what you can do to be better the next day. An ability to quickly recover from a setback can help you juggle your workload and still come out with your mental health intact.

## The Problem with Multitasking and Productivity

Here is a scenario: let's say that you decided to handle 3 tasks for 3 clients at once (because you procrastinated on starting). One task has you create a blog post, another has you handle a Facebook handle, and another has you designing some graphics for a web marketing campaign. All of these tasks have to be done by 5 P.M. that day.

And let's assume that you managed to complete all tasks by sundown. Now, ask yourself this question: which of those tasks has a quality that you are satisfied with the most? There is a chance that you can't pick any of the three. You might not even remember in which order you managed to complete all three tasks.

The truth with multitasking is that it is one of the most difficult mental feats to achieve for any normal person. Focusing on something takes up quite an amount of our mental energy. The more difficult a task is, the more focus is needed to get things right. What makes multitasking problematic is that it demands from you to focus on more than one thing at any given instance. The mental drain is even more pronounced the more you switch from task to task.

Going back to the scenario above, it is most likely that you have already tired yourself out before the 5 P.M. mark. This is because the three tasks done simultaneously have depleted your brain of whatever mental energy it has. Chances are that at least one of the tasks you finished was really a rough draft instead of a final draft, and you're just hoping to scrape by without the client putting up too much of a fuss.

## Sacrificing Accuracy and Creativity

What exactly happens to your work when you multitask? The most obvious effect is that you tend to commit more mistakes. Switching from task to task causes your brain to do a bit of backtracking to figure out where it left off in that particular activity. And when it does this, the potential for error increases. For instance, you might forget a crucial detail for that task or skip a process or two because you are hurrying.

Multitasking also affects your creativity. Creativity is often produced when the brain can follow one particular trail of thought and ideas. If it has to hop from one trail to another, it tends to rely on safer and blander solutions. At the end of the day, you end up with three haphazardly done, derivative tasks. You could have excelled more if you chose to focus on one.

## The Art of Monotasking

Instead of Multitasking, you should do Monotasking. This is where you pool in all your mental energies to focus on completing tasks one after another instead of simultaneously doing them all. Many freelancers that I work with swear by monotasking, working on one project per day. Rachael, a freelance copywriter, shared that she writes for one project a day, and ends her day by brainstorming for another project. That way she gets a little variety, but doesn't push herself to create the same output for both clients in one day.

You might think that this is impossible on particularly hectic days. However, even half an hour of hyper-focusing on your work can achieve so much more than frantically hopping from one task to another. Here's how:

## Remove All Temptations to Multitask

Anything that is unrelated to the task at hand should be set aside until you finish it. If you are not scheduled for some Social Media Optimization work until noon, for example, then close off all tabs that will require you to check on Facebook or Twitter. If your graphic design task is not due to start until 3 P.M., then don't run your design programs while you are still completing your blog post.

Multitasking temptations don't even have to be related to any work you were contracted to perform. The people around you might ask you to perform some tasks themselves. If possible, put up a "Do Not Disturb" sign at your workplace. This way, your friends and family would not bother you about anything that is not close to an emergency.

## The ONE Screen Rule

Now I'm not talking about having multiple monitors. The one screen you should be looking at is the one on your workplace computer.

Other screens like the one coming from your mobile device or your TV must be set aside or turned off. This way, the only bright thing with moving text and images that is demanding your attention will be the screen of your computer.

## Set Your Priorities

Which of the tasks should you do one after the other? You have some options here. The first option is to sort them by urgency. Essentially, if all of them must be sent that day, which of your tasks has to be sent the earliest? The ones with an earlier deadline will be done first and the rest will follow.

Going back to the situation above, if the blog posts are due by noon, then common sense dictates that you focus all of your energies on finishing them before lunchtime. If the SMO and graphic design tasks are to be sent by 4 pm and 8 pm respectively, that will leave you with enough time after noontime to focus on them.

The other option is to prioritize them by the degree of difficulty. The tasks that will demand the most focus and deplete a lot of mental strength will have to be finished first.

In the example above, it is quite apparent that graphic design takes the most out of your mental energies so it has to be done first. The next to follow will be the blog post and the last will be the social media activities.

## Schedule

If you choose the second option mentioned above, you must still determine how much time you can devote to finishing the task. You cannot have it take too much time as it will deplete your mental energies. Somewhere in between 4 to 6 hours for the heavier tasks should suffice. As for the lighter tasks, that work period should be in between 2 to 4 hours.

Again, this is all dependent on your daily schedule. Some days allow you to be lenient with your scheduling. And then there are days when you have just to bear with the crunch. When everything is on a deadline, you have to be as quick and accurate as possible with your work so you could move on to your other tasks.

## Hunker Down

After all, has been planned, what is left to do is for you to implement all the strategies above. You must commit to your schedule so that you can finish all the tasks in time without sacrificing quality. Your ability to ignore all distractions and maintain that hyper-focused state of mind will be crucial here.

If everything is properly done, you should be able to reach the end of the day with all tasks satisfactorily completed. Now, you could proceed to take your rest or attend to your matters. You are the boss of your time, after all.

## Being Productive on a Hectic Day at Work

Multitasking becomes more of a temptation if you find yourself having to deal with multiple deadlines in a single day. Can you avoid such a scenario? Normally, the answer is yes and proper scheduling can help you avoid having to deal with this situation.

However, there might come a time when you have no say in the matter. Perhaps clients want to have things done ASAP and you can't wriggle yourself out of the agreement. Perhaps there was a power outage yesterday and you have a considerable amount of tasks backlogged that must be completed immediately.

The point is there might come a time when the universe would pull a sick prank on you and just dump quite a lot of work on your lap. There's no avoiding this because the situation is already developing. Your ability to adapt to the changing schedules and demands will be important here.

However, the worst thing that you can do is to attempt to do two or more tasks at any given hour. It's next to impossible to pull off and you are setting yourself up for failure. And do remember that the goal here is to please your clients with quality output so they would continue paying you generously for your efforts.

Think of it like those Predator movies of the past. Like the titular alien of that franchise, your chances of surviving in the jungle of remote work and producing quality output increase the quicker you learn to take out your challenges one by one.

## Chapter Five Action Steps

- What does your perfect Freelance/Entrepreneur schedule look like?

  ○ What do you do first thing in the morning?

  ○ What do you do mid-morning?

  ○ What do you do early afternoon?

  ○ What do you do late afternoon?

  ○ What do you do in the evening?

- What does Monday look like? Tuesday? Wednesday? Thursday? Friday?

  ○ Do you work on the weekend?

- What time do you take breaks?

  ○ Exercise?

  ○ Eat?

  ○ Spend time with family?

  ○ Hobbies?

- How can you break up your workdays to avoid multi-tasking?

  - One project in the morning and one in the afternoon?

  - Divide projects based on what part of the creation process each is in? For example, maybe you are editing a final draft for one project, writing a chapter for a second project, and brainstorming for a third project?

# 6

— • —

# MASTERING YOUR SCHEDULE AND ROUTINE

W ould you consider yourself a morning person, an afternoon achiever, or a night owl?

When and where are you most productive?

As a freelancer or entrepreneur, when will you get the bulk of
your work done?

How will you fit leisure time into your schedule?

Are you prepared to create a daily, weekly, and monthly
schedule and stick to it?

These are all questions you'll need to navigate as your own
boss.

## First Things First

One of the first things you'll need to iron out as a successful
freelancer is a daily routine. Some people hate that word and
prefer to be spontaneous. However, a successful freelancer or
entrepreneur will tell you that the key to a flourishing career is

a schedule. This includes getting a full night of restful sleep, a structured morning checklist, and a nutritious breakfast.

It's confusing how we have more time to work when we're working from home, but it often feels like we have less time. It is a little mind-boggling when we're used to working in an office or onsite with people all around us, but now we have to set our own boundaries. Time is a precious commodity when you work from home. You suddenly have all the time in the world, but it's also spread out so thin that it feels like you don't have any at all. It's ironic because you're no longer confined to a certain space and time, but you still have to manage your time carefully or else the day will slip away from you.

We often think that staying at for the entire day is more productive, but that's not always the case. The freedom to work from home can be a curse if we're not careful about how we spend our time. Just because we have all this time doesn't mean that we can sit and be comfortable, nor just work straight through and not take breaks.

## Leniency Leads to Laziness

There's a reason we're usually not productive when working from home. It's because we've been given too much leniency and it often leads to laziness. We can be in our pajamas all day, take breaks whenever we want, and work at our own pace.

The problem with this type of work arrangement is that it's easy to get used to and very comfortable. Before we know it, we've fallen into a trap of being unproductive because there are no real consequences for our actions.

The key to avoiding this pitfall is to be mindful of our surroundings and the level of comfort we're in. We need to set boundaries for ourselves so that we don't fall into a trap of being too comfortable.

The same distractions that we face in an office can also occur when working from home, such as family members popping in or wanting to chat, the lure of the laundry or dishes calling our name, or just getting lost in a project and not realizing how much time has passed.

## Structure leads to SUCCESS

Just because we're at home doesn't mean that we can slack off and not work.

Intentionally structuring your morning can make or break your entire day- it sets the tone. For example, my freelance friend Ryan always walks her dog, makes coffee, and begins her day with her most urgent project. Ryan is the most productive first thing, so she wants to use her most productive time for her most demanding work instead of wasting it on emails. She intentionally answers emails at the end of her workday. In the same way, she structures her week so that Monday - Thursday she is working on her client projects, and Fridays she is working on her business. So, on Fridays, she researches and pitches new clients, completes coursework, updates her website and social media accounts, and goes over her calendar.

Jon starts his morning by getting his kids ready for school as he listens to NPR and makes breakfast. He likes to connect and ease into his day, without diving into the pile on his desk first thing. Once the kids are out the door he goes for a jog, takes a shower, and sits down at his desk no later than 9 A.M. to review the daily goals he set the night before. Jon likes to respond to emails first thing as well as send invoices or handle other small business, and dives into his projects around 10:30. Around 3:30 he transitions from whatever project he is working on to working on his business or checking his email again. His kids are home by 4:30 P.M. at which time his workday is done, and he transitions into dad mode again.

How you spend your morning can make or break your entire day. If you want to have a productive day, you need to have a structure in place that begins the moment your feet hit the ground. And you need to execute this plan Every. Single. Day.

Now, this does not mean you need to get up at 6 A.M. or struggle through a complicated project first thing before the coffee has kicked in. Maybe you choose to start your morning with exercise, responding to emails, and writing out your tasks because you do your best work after 10 A.M. Maybe your morning is waking up at noon, eating a bowl of Kashi cereal, going to the gym, and tackling your large projects in the evening when everyone else is winding down. Or maybe you split up your day, finishing some work before lunch and some work in the afternoon before your kids get off the bus and your spouse walks in the door.

The "morning", whatever time of day that is for you, is not important. The KEY is having a consistent routine that leads to productive work. As a freelancer, you need to take control of your schedule instead of letting it control you. Creating a daily routine and sticking to it is a way of ensuring a productive day. Psychologist and occupational health expert, Emma Mardlin says "People who have a set routine tend to be more productive because they're not wasting time working out what they should do next. When we have a plan and know what we are supposed to be doing, it is easier to stay focused and avoid procrastination. Having a routine also gives us a sense of control over our day and our lives, which can be very empowering."

Experts suggest that it takes about 21 days to form a new habit. Habits start to form when we do something consistently for a period of time. So, if you want to make your daily routine a habit, start by doing it for 21 days straight. After that, it should become a natural part of you.

## Setting up your daily schedule for success

The freelancers I work with typically fall into two categories when planning a successful work day. Ryan, for example, likes to review each upcoming work week on Sunday and sketch out a preliminary plan for the week with daily goals. She then will revisit her goals at the end of each day, adjusting as needed to account for meetings with clients, last-minute requests from clients, and revisions to projects.

Jon, on the other hand, likes to review his priorities every morning. He has told me the key to winning the day is to start with a couple of easy wins that he can accomplish without much time invested, giving him the umph to tackle the larger projects that need more of his time and attention.

Susan, a freelance life coach, likes to block her time. For example, she only schedules meetings and phone calls on Tuesdays, Wednesdays, and Saturdays. Mondays and Thursdays she gets the majority of her writing, researching, and emailing done. She loves knowing that Mondays and Thursdays are focused primarily on writing while connecting with clients via face-to-face time occupies the rest of her work week.

How will you determine what your top priorities are for the day? When do you like to plan for your workday- the night before or the morning of? Do you keep a running to-do list or do you make a new one each day?

As a freelancer, part of your workday will include writing a to-do list and making goals. Some of the most effective to-do list templates include the Eisenhower Matrix, the Ivy Lee Method, and the Pomodoro Technique.

The **Eisenhower Matrix** is a time management tool that helps you prioritize tasks by urgency and importance. It is done by creating a list of all your tasks and then categorizing them into four quadrants:

1. Quadrant one is for urgent and important tasks that need to be done immediately.

2. Quadrant two is for important tasks that are not urgent and can be scheduled.

3. Quadrant three is for urgent but not important tasks that can be delegated.

4. Quadrant four is for tasks that are neither urgent nor important and can be eliminated.

The **Ivy Lee Method** is a to-do list method that involves writing down six tasks you need to do tomorrow and then ranking them in order of importance. You then work on the first task until it is complete before moving on to the next one.

This method is effective as it allows you to focus on one task at a time and avoid getting overwhelmed by a long list of tasks.

The **Pomodoro Technique** is a time management technique that helps you break down work into 25-minute intervals, separated by five-minute breaks. After four intervals, you take a longer break of 15-30 minutes.

Finally, part of your workday will include scheduled breaks. Ryan, Jon, and Susan all shared that they take regular breaks to maintain productivity and focus. Ryan sets a timer for 50 minutes every time she sits down to work. She focuses for the fifty minutes, then takes a ten-minute stretch break, goes to the bathroom, refills her water bottle, and does some gentle yoga. She DOES NOT check her email- it is so easy to get sidetracked by email, Ryan swears by the habit of only checking her email the last hour of her workday.

Jon likes to work in two-hour blocks, and then take a half-hour break where he does some chores around the house to move his body and get away from the computer.

Susan uses the timer on her phone to keep track of her work blocks. She starts her timer as soon as she sits down to work. Instead of scheduled breaks, she allows herself a break whenever she wants. However, she stops the timer on her phone. No matter how many breaks she takes during the day, she works for seven hours on writing days, and nine hours on Tuesdays and Wednesdays, with Saturday being a half day, using her phone to keep track.

Aside from organizing your tasks, it is also important to take breaks in between work. Working for long periods of time can lead to fatigue and make us less productive, especially when we're staring at the computer. Taking regular breaks can help improve our focus and energy levels.

You will be in charge of your time, which means keeping yourself accountable but not running yourself ragged. At the beginning of your freelance/entreprenuer journey, it may be difficult for you to manage your time. It's okay to try different routines and structures to find what works for you! And guess what- when you nail your schedule, it'll be like when Cinderella slipped on that glass slipper and rode off into the sunset.

## Work to Live. Not live to work.

We work to live, not live to work. It is important to remember that we should not sacrifice our health and well-being for productivity. Working too much can lead to burnout, which is a state of physical, mental, and emotional exhaustion. As a freelancer or entrepreneur, you may have to work outside the traditional 9-5 hours or find yourself working more than 40 hours a week when your business is first getting off the ground. This, unfortunately, is normal.

While we grind to meet deadlines and achieve our goals, we must not forget to take care of ourselves. We can do this by eating healthy meals, exercising regularly, focusing on quality in our relationships with friends and family, enjoying hobbies, and getting enough sleep. Doing things we enjoy can help reduce work-related stress and increase our overall happiness.

As you begin creating your routine and weekly schedule, think about how you're going to create a work-life balance. How will you ensure you have enough time for both your work life and your personal life? When we have a good balance, we are more likely to be productive at work as we are not stressed about other aspects of our life. A balanced life will save us from burnout which can lead to a decrease in productivity as well as other negative effects on our health such as anxiety, depression, and insomnia.

It is also important to note that productivity is not always about working more. In fact, working too much can lead to burnout and actually make us less productive. It is important to find a balance between work and leisure time.

Some ways to keep ourselves healthy when feeling drained from work can be a take short walks, meditate, or even just take a few deep breaths. It is also necessary that we remember to stay hydrated and eat healthy meals. Foods that are good for your mental health including omega-rich foods, dark chocolate, and green tea should always be on your grocery list.

We should also avoid working (and social media) right before we go to sleep, as this can disrupt our sleep schedule and make it harder to wake up in the morning. Irregular sleeping patterns may lead to serious health problems in the long run such as obesity, heart disease, and diabetes.

It is salient to have a set routine before bedtime in order to relax our mind and body for sleep. This can include reading a book, writing in a journal, or stretching your body. Doing this will help signal to our brain that it is time to wind down for the day and prepare for sleep. Steer clear of using electronics such as phones or laptops in bed as the blue light emitted from screens can prevent us from falling asleep.

To sum it up, being productive does not mean working yourself to death. It is about finding a balance between work and leisure time and taking care of your physical and mental health.

Creating a healthy routine for yourself is the key to maintaining productivity levels throughout the day.

## The Yin Yang of Productivity

Balance is the key when it comes to productivity. With the right amount of work and leisure time, we can find the perfect equilibrium for a productive day.

A noteworthy saying goes, "All work and no play makes Jack a dull boy." This means that too much work and no leisure time can make us bored and uninterested. On the other hand, if we have too much free time and not enough work, we can become unmotivated.

The perfect balance between work and leisure time is essential for a productive day. This balance can be different for everyone, and it is important to find what works best for you. We should not strive to be productive every single hour of the day as this is simply impossible and unsustainable. Instead, we should focus on being productive when we have the most energy, and focus, or when it matters most (like during client meetings) and taking breaks when we need them.

## Structure Your Leisure Time

What do you do when you're not working? This is your leisure time to spend as you see fit. Ryan is working on a novel in her leisure time, Jon likes working on projects around the house (currently he is building a deck) and spending time with his kids and wife, and Susan loves to watch funny TikTok videos and share them with her daughter and mother. All three purposely structure leisure time into their day because they all agreed that if left to their own devices, they would work and work and work.

You don't have to have to earn money just to be productive all day long. Self-improvement and happiness are worthwhile goals, too. Not only do they make you happier, but leisure activities also give your brain downtime and allow your work to flourish.

## Always Have Time to do NOTHING

Burnout remains a fairly huge issue when doing remote work. All that constant need to focus can be draining on your mind and body. There might be some days so hectic that whatever mental energy you replenished over the night won't be enough for the next day.

This is why it is recommended for your brain take a breather in between tasks. To do this, have some time in the day when you are supposed to do nothing or, at least, not obligated to do something. This is your "Nothing" period and it is the best set immediately after a shift.

So, does that mean that you have to do absolutely nothing in these periods? Yes and No. You can do nothing, of course, but that does not mean that you can't do anything. Perhaps you might want to play a game on your phone or check your social media pages. Jon vacuums or puts laundry away; Ryan does Yoga or stares at her birdfeeders for a minute.

What this period is for is to let your mind get the break that it needs. Unless there is an emergency, the Nothing period should not be spent on doing calls for clients, making amendments to reports, or checking up on company emails. If possible, get away from your phone and computer, and give your eyes a break from looking at screens.

These periods of doing unfocused work (like laundry) or resting could be anywhere from ten to thirty minutes, whatever amount of time it takes to relax from hectic activity. Don't go so long that you are unmotivated to continue with work, though. Freelance friends tell me that they can get sucked into social media for hours and then put off finishing goals they made for the day.

It's confusing how we have more time to work when we're working from home, but it often feels like we have less time. It is a little boggling when we're used to working in an office or onsite with people all around us, but now we have to set our own boundaries.

## Managing Time When Working from Home

Start by figuring out when are the most productive. For some people, it's in the morning, for others, it's in the evening. Work with our natural rhythm as much as possible to maximize our productivity. To some, this may mean getting up early to work before the family wakes up, or working late into the night after everyone has gone to bed. If we find that we're not as productive during certain times of the day, try to adjust our schedule accordingly.

Creating a schedule is not an exact science, so be prepared to make some adjustments along the way. But by being mindful of our time and what we need to be productive, we can make the most of our work-from-home situation!

## Time Blocking

A readily crafted schedule will help us manage our time more efficiently when working from home. Just like in an office, it's important to break down our day into chunks and assign specific tasks to each chunk of time. This will help us stay on track and avoid distractions.

Block off time for specific tasks. For example, if you know that you need two hours to work on a project, block off those two hours in your schedule and don't let anything else interfere. This will help to ensure that you're productive and that your time is used efficiently. A task checker can be used as a physical or digital reminder of what we are working on and when we are scheduled to work on it. This will help keep us accountable and prevent distractions from derailing our train of thought.

# Bite-sized Chunks

Working from home can be a great way to get more done, but only if we're mindful of our time. Slicing the day into manageable chunks and scheduling specific tasks to those time slots will help us stay on track and be more productive.

When working on long-term projects, we may specify working on it for a certain number of hours each day, or until it's completed. This will help us stay focused and avoid distractions.

But even when we're not working on a long-term project, chunking our time into 30 or 60-minute intervals can be helpful in avoiding distractions and being more productive. Divide and conquer!

# Time Management Tools

Aside from various techniques to help us manage our time, there are also tools that we can use to be more productive. Apps such as RescueTime can help us track how we're spending our time and what apps or websites we're using the most. This information can then be used to help us create a more effective schedule. With the details of the projects, websites, and apps we're using, time-tracking apps can help us better understand how we work and where our time is going.

There are several apps for time management, including Toggl, which tracks time spent on specific tasks, and Focus Booster, which uses the Pomodoro technique to break up work into 25 minutes intervals with a five-minute break in between.

By using some of these tools and techniques, we can help manage our time more effectively when working from home!

## Handling the Inevitable Distractions

Working from home can often lead to distractions. Dogs need to be walked, children may need help with their homework, and the list goes on.

Instead of letting these distractions derail us, we should try to incorporate them into our schedule. If we know that we have a break coming up soon, then we can work on a task for a little bit and then take a break to walk the dog or help our children with their homework. By incorporating these distractions into our schedule, we can still stay productive while working from home.

## Embrace What's Infront of You

Accepting and making the most of the distractions that come with working from home will not only help us stay productive, but it can also be fun.

It is what it is. There's no need to fight it. Working from home has its own set of distractions and we should embrace them.

Instead of piling up the frustrations of working from home, let's take a step back and enjoy the distractions that come with it. We may include our parental and pet duties as distractions, but there are other activities that we can enjoy as well.

We can take a break and watch our favorite show, read a book, work on a hobby, or even take a nap. Embracing the distractions that come with working from home can make the experience more enjoyable.

## Hypothesize and Experiment

Don't be scared to experiment with different techniques and tools that can help us manage our time when working from home and increase our production output. If something isn't working for us, then we can always change it up. We may need to try a few different things before we find what works best for us. Mix and match apps and techniques to see what helps us stay focused and on track.

The most important thing is that we remain flexible and are willing to experiment with different things. This will help us find what works best for us and increase our productivity when working from home.

# Chapter Six Action Steps

- When are you at your most productive? How can you set your schedule so that you're always working at prime productive time?

- What is a morning work routine that you can put into place...

  - What will you do first thing every morning?

    - Check email? Make a to-do list? Respond to calls? Schedule meetings? Dig right in to your most urgent work?

  - What is a midday work routine that you can put into place?

  - What is an end-of-work-day routine that you can put into place?

  - Design your perfect work schedule. Test it for a week. If something doesn't go well, make adjustments as needed.

  - What are disruptions that you need to account for or work into your schedule?

  - How will you arrange and manage your time?

# 7

## DESIGNING A PRODUCTIVE WORKSPACE AT HOME

We talked about this briefly in Chapter 2, but your workspace can either support your productivity or destroy it. For example, I am easily distracted by sound. Therefore, when I work, my space needs to be silent. Robert, one of my neighbors, doesn't like working in complete silence. He always has the radio or TV going quietly as he's working. Jon can't work when his kids are home, because he found they would constantly interrupt his flow when he was in the middle of a project. Ryan discovered that she can't sit next to the window or in an unsupportive chair after she started having back problems.

Creating the ideal work environment is one of the first steps to ensuring your success as a freelancer or entrepreneur. Stepping out of our usual office space and into our homes can be quite a jarring experience. It's not just the change of scenery, but also the potential for new distractions that can make it difficult to get work done from home. Challenges such as maintaining concentration, ensuring ergonomics, and avoiding distractions can threaten our productivity and freelance careers.

But every difficulty in adjusting to our new work environments presents an opportunity to learn and grow. If we can take the time to create a productive work environment at home, we can come out of this experience not just surviving, but thriving.

## Setting up your remote location for success

If your idea of remote work is just sitting anywhere at home and then booting up your computer, you are setting yourself up for failure. Kelly started quarantine working in her recliner in front of the TV, and quickly found her productivity dwindling. Remember that structure is what separates an office from your home setting so introducing that element to your workspace is going to be crucial.

Creating a productive work environment is like repotting a plant. We need to find a place for our work that is conducive to growth. In the same way, we need to find an environment at home that will allow us to be productive.

If possible, dedicate an entire room where you can work. This gives you the option to shut yourself off from the rest of the house if you want to and also store your work-related documents and equipment. If it's not possible to dedicate an entire room as your workspace, choose a corner where you have access to two walls and can hang a calendar, whiteboard or corkboard, sticky note reminders, etc. Freelancers Susan and Ryan both set up offices in corners of their apartment bedrooms for a desk and workspace. Both women spend time working at the library or coffee shop as well.

In case there are no available rooms in the house, we can create a space in another area where we can be productive. This may be a spot in the living room near a window where we can set up our laptops and get some work done.

The important thing is to find a place where we feel comfortable working and that is large enough for us to have all of the materials that we need.

We may choose one that is far from the television or other common areas in the house where people congregate. We may also want to make sure that there is good lighting and ventilation.

Placement is also important here. For example, your living or family room is not the most ideal location as it places you at the very center of the house. You're in a rather vulnerable spot to all forms of distraction- and if I'm being honest, I wouldn't want to have extended family or friends over and in my workspace. I don't know about you, but my mom is nosy. She would be poking through all my work stuff the moment my back was turned.

Ventilation is also important as too much discomfort can also ruin your concentration. Have your workspace set near a window (as long as it's not too distracting or the sun is in your eyes the entire day) and invest in good air conditioning.

## The Right Tools

Like a plant being repotted to foreign soil, we need the right tools for our new environment to make the adjustment seamless. The same is true for our work when transitioning to working at home.

Just as we would have our office supplies with us when working in an office, we need to have our home supplies with us when working at home. This includes having a good chair, a desk that is at the right height, a comfortable place to sit, and good lighting. Our documents and supplies within easy reach.

In addition, we may stick a corkboard on the wall near our work area and post to-do lists, inspiration, or pictures of things that motivate us. This will give us easy access to what we need to stay on task.With the right tools for our transition, we can create a productive work environment at home that promotes ease and flow the way our office space used to.

## Economic but Ergonomic

It is also highly suggested that we set up our workstation ergonomically. This includes having a comfortable chair, a desk that is the right height, and making sure that our computer monitor is at eye level.

In addition to finding a suitable place to work, we also need to take care of our ergonomics. This is important not just for comfort but also for preventing injuries.

We can start by making sure that our chair provides adequate support for our back and that our monitor is at the correct height. It is also important to have a good keyboard and mouse to use. We may want to consider using an ergonomic keyboard and mouse to help reduce strain on our hands and wrists.

Once we have our space set up, we can then focus on developing the habits and routines that will help us to stay productive.

As for personalization, just make sure that whatever is on your desk should motivate you towards completing your tasks. Things like reminders, quotes, and even pictures of your family should be enough to help your mind focus.

If done right, you should have a workspace that reflects your priorities and gets you psyched up for completing your tasks. All that is left for you to do is to stick to the schedule and get things done on time.

## Rules, Roles, Rolls

Another important aspect of creating a productive work environment at home is to establish some ground rules for roommates, partners, family members, and children. Let everyone in the home know the hours you are working, and/or post a note on the door to alert everyone not to interrupt. For example, Robert keeps a red Stop Sign on his door for his kids. When its on the door, they can only interrupt him if they're dying or the house is on fire. When the Stop Sign is not on the door, the kids can interrupt if they need something.  It is very important to enforce this boundary with family. Share that they will help you be successful if they let you focus on work during work hours.

Other rules for children and remote working include not interrupting us when we are in meetings, keeping their toys away from our work area, and not coming into our office without knocking. Having some set rules in place will help to create a productive work environment at home as well as set clear expectations for your children. Ryan's kids needed practice with the expectations, but now protect their mom's worktime and keep their friends in-line when they come over to play.

## Make Housekeeping a Part of Your Daily Schedule

The first casualty of embracing the remote work life is always the cleanliness of your house. What you may not have realized is that the overall cleanliness of your living and working space can affect your mood. In turn, your mood can affect your willingness to complete your tasks.

So, for the sake of becoming productive, you might as well devote a portion of your time to cleaning your house. Take the time to clean your desk and take out whatever trash was made from the previous day. You can also perform cleaning rituals at the end of your work day. Jon, the freelance worker I mentioned in the previous chapter, likes to take breaks from his computer to clean and straighten his house, getting chores done while also relaxing his mind.

Housekeeping helps you become productive in two ways. First, it improves the overall organization of your workspace which makes it more conducive to productivity. Second, a cleaning habit further reinforces a work structure at home. Think of it this way: cleaning your home is already a worthwhile achievement. If you can do that every day without nobody telling you to do so, then you subconsciously tell yourself that you can finish your tasks without supervision.

## Circumvent to Stay Efficient

Avoid distractions as much as possible, such as the TV or the internet. If we can't completely avoid them, then try to limit the amount of time we spend on them.

Working from home definitely has its perks, but it can also be a distraction. It's easy to get side-tracked when there are no real consequences for our actions.

We can try to circumvent these distractions by working in a quiet and distraction-free environment. This can be difficult to do when we're used to working in a noisy office, but it's important to try and create an atmosphere that is conducive to productivity.

Putting on headphones can help create this type of environment, as well as avoid checking social media or watching TV.

One common challenge every working individual faces is distractions. Whether your a CEO or an entry-level employee, it is likely that at some point you will be interrupted while trying to

get work done. In an office setting, distractions are usually han-
dled by the individual who is being bothered. They will either
politely ask the person to stop or they will move to another part
of the office where they are less likely to be bothered.

When working from home, distractions can be a bit more
difficult to manage. It's easy for people to come into our homes
without realizing that we're actually working or for us to get
distracted by the television or the internet.

## Modulation

Distraction will always be around the four corners of our lives,
however, we can manage it by regulating our environment and
how we spend our time. Start by politely requesting all parties at
home to be respectful of your work time, and if needed put on
headphones so you can't hear them. If the TV is a distraction,
try working in an area where it's not possible to see or hear it.

The more we focus on our work, the less likely we are to be
disturbed by outside elements. And eventually, we will become
so engrossed in our work that distractions will have little to no
effect on us.

## Postulation

It is important to remember that when working from home, the
boundaries between our personal and professional lives become
blurred. This means that we have to be more conscious of how

we're spending our time and make sure that we're not getting too carried away with non-work activities.

Affirm the fact that when we work from home, it doesn't mean that we're on vacation. We still have to put in the effort and make sure that we're productive. Although it may be more difficult to stay focused when working from home, with a bit of discipline, it is definitely possible.

## Assertion

No distraction will ever be completely eliminated, however, asserting that a day's work is finished will end the distraction. In any office setting, there are bound to be distractions. Whether it's a colleague who is constantly talking or the sound of typing in the background, these distractions can be a bit disruptive when we're trying to focus on our work.

Although it's impossible to eliminate all distractions, we can try to mitigate them by setting boundaries. For example, if we know that we only have an hour to work on a project, then we're less likely to be disturbed by outside elements.

Another way to deal with distractions is by acknowledging them and moving on. It's important not to dwell on them and instead focus on the task at hand.

Staying productive when working from home can be a bit of a challenge, but with a bit of effort, skills, and self-discipline, it can definitely be done.

Working from home can often lead to distractions. Dogs need to be walked, children may need help with their homework, and the list goes on. Instead of letting these distractions derail us, we should try to incorporate them into our schedule. If we know that we have a break coming up soon, then we can work on a task for a little bit and then take a break to walk the dog or help our children with their homework.

By incorporating these distractions into our schedule, we can still stay productive while working from home.

## Chapter Seven Action Steps

- What can you do to ensure a productive workspace at home?

- How can you make your workspace healthy?

  ○ Standing desk?

  ○ Supportive chair?

  ○ Great lighting?

  ○ Air Purifier?

  ○ Multiple monitors?

- How can you eliminate distractions?

- What rules and boundaries do you need to make for your children, partner, roommates, and/or co-workers?

# 8

---•---

# BUILDING HEALTHY RELATIONSHIPS AS A REMOTE WORKER

T rent never dreamed that one of the hardest aspects of working remotely and as a freelancer would be forging relationships with his co-workers, clients, supervisors, and vendors as well as maintaining healthy relationships with his partner and family. In fact, when weighing whether to enter the freelance world, he never took relationships into account at all.

This is where many remote workers and freelancers make a mistake.

For example, introverted freelancers believe that the stress of relationships will lessen when moving to the remote or freelance world- but that's not true. In fact, many workers find that they have to work *harder* to establish themselves as experts, communicate through email, contribute and collaborate on projects (even freelancers get hired to work with others- copywriters and graphic designers work together all the time, for example), maintain boundaries, and keep the communication going.

Are you flexible and responsive to the needs of your clients?
What if a client wants to have weekly Zoom meetings with
updates about the project? Can you provide update emails as
much or little as a client wants? Will you download and learn
new collaboration apps like Slack to get hired for projects? Are
you willing to constantly learn new technology? Because all of
the above is part of becoming a freelancer or entrepreneur. All
clients will have different communication needs.

Not only that, when you are working from home, you need to
be able to communicate boundaries, rules, responsibilities, etc.
with your roommates, partner, children, and extended family.

Why is communication so important? What does this look
like? Let's start by looking at our work relationships.

## Building and Maintaining Healthy Relationships with Clients, Supervisors, and Co-Workers

Working away from a company's stakeholders in a remote setup
is one of the challenges freelancers face. Aside from the technological requirements, we need to be conscientious of the manner
by which we build and maintain our relationships with our
remote co-workers, especially if we are working with people
in different time zones or cultures. But just as we would in
an office environment, we should aim to create a positive and
productive relationship with our remote counterparts. We can

do this by taking the time to get to know them, building trust, and communicating effectively.

## Work Provides Access to Built-in Relationships

Any business or company requires some form of human interaction to succeed. Whether it is the relationship between a manager and their team, or customer service and their clients, relationships are key to any business operation.

Good people skills are a must if we want to maintain healthy relationships with our virtual co-workers and collaborators. By nourishing our bonds with our co-workers, even on virtual platforms, we are building networks vital for the success of the project. Healthy relationships make a workplace happier and more conducive to productivity which boosts people's morale, creativity, and effectiveness.

## Start by Communicating

Like in any relationship outside our work titles, good communication, and mutual respect are the cornerstones to a trusting and lasting collaboration. Distance does not mean we can't communicate effectively. In fact, we might need to be more deliberate in our communication with remote co-workers. These miles apart from our distant colleagues can be bridged with healthy and effective communication.

What does this look like? For freelancer Ryan, this means sending weekly or biweekly email updates about the stage of the project she is working on to her clients as well as sharing the work with them, complementing the work, and specifically mentioning the challenges she is untangling. Jon works with international clients and a supervisor who prefers to communicate face-to-face, so he schedules weekly zoom meetings to check in. Now, the cool thing about the zoom meeting is that these meetings rarely last more than twenty minutes.

As a freelancer, a full 25% of your work time may be spent communicating via email, Zoom, Slack, Google docs, or whatever other platforms you use with clients, co-workers, and bosses. As an entrepreneur, even more time will be spent on building relationships- with potential clients and investors!

Effective communication takes practice. Are you flexible to communicate in a way that your clients prefer? If you refuse to Zoom, that may limit your client base. Are you willing to take the time to write daily update emails? Update a shared work calendar? Contribute and collaborate during online meetings or on a collaborative app like Slack?

## Work Language

Productivity and cohesive work are essential in any organization, especially when working remotely. By taking the time to build healthy relationships with our virtual co-workers, we are creating a more positive and productive work environment.

Take the time to comment when your co-worker shares that she got a new puppy; speak up during meetings and offer collaborative suggestions that reduce the workload for everyone. Participate during ice breakers. Not only do we benefit from having happy employees, but our company reaps the rewards of a cohesive and well-functioning team.

Sometimes, work language is not a spoken language, but rather a form of communication such as emojis, GIFs, or abbreviations. As long as we are all on the same page with the meaning of these, they can be a great way to communicate efficiently.

## Diverse People, Common Goal

How we deal with differences can make or break our relationships with them.

Working virtually means working with people of diverse ages, backgrounds, and cultures. Some of our co-workers are younger or older than us which can present a challenge in a remote setup. Some of them weigh things, actions, language, and words differently than we do. It is essential that before anything else, we take the time to learn about their culture and what is important to them. With this information, we can avoid any cultural clashes and work together in a productive manner.

We should be mindful of our words and actions, especially when communicating with those who are from different cultures than us. We need to remember that just because we are working remotely, doesn't mean we can forget about the basic principles of humans - respect and understanding. Hence, we should not let this diversity hinder our relationships with our remote co-workers. In order to stay connected, we need to make an effort to connect with them on a personal level. We can do this by sharing photos, articles, or just general news about our lives outside of work.

Diversity is an opportunity, not a challenge. With a little effort, we can use this diversity to our advantage and create a more productive and positive work environment. We often take for granted the relationships we have with our co-workers in the office. But, with so many people working remotely, it's more important than ever to focus on our relationships with them.

## Cultivate Rapport

Maintaining a healthy relationship with our coworkers in a remote work setup requires effective communication. Unlike our office setup that we can physically see and interact with, our remote co-workers can be faceless entities. This can make it difficult to build trust and communication. A full 55 percent of human communication happens through body language; so, when you take body language out of the equation, think about how difficult that is on relationships.

Trent realized that he communicated a lot using humor and sarcasm, which coworkers had a hard time picking up on because there is no sarcastic font, lol. This was really brought to his attention when a client from a different culture asked pointed questions about an email he had sent. Trent had no bad intentions, and was, in fact, trying to build rapport by using humor, but that didn't come across to his client. He realized he needed to adjust his communication style; his jokes fell flat when no one could see his face.

## The Basics Still Apply

Aside from keeping a positive attitude, taking time to learn about our co-workers, and being socially inclined, the basic rules and principles of communication still apply.

## Listen actively.

This includes actively listening, being patient, and not interrupting. We should also avoid sending multiple messages at once, as this can be overwhelming and cause our colleagues to miss something important.

Provide time to listen. Remember, just like in an office setting, not everyone is at their desk all the time. We should allow ample time for our colleagues to reply to our messages, and avoid bombarding them with messages throughout the day.

## Speak to the Common Idea

We need to remember that we are working with people from different lands or time zones and that they may not understand sarcasm or jokes. So, it's always a good idea to avoid them or explain their meaning if we feel they are necessary.

We must be extra careful with our words and actions, as even the tone of a sentence can be easily misinterpreted when all communication is done through text or email. Take an extra second to read over your message to see if it could be interpreted poorly.

## Correspondence is Key

Just as in a regular office, establishing a good rapport with our virtual co-workers is essential for a healthy and productive relationship.

Keeping the culture of formal correspondence thru emails, chats and the occasional call will help to keep everyone in check. This also helps when it comes time for reviews and appraisals as all correspondences are documented and any misunderstandings can be clarified with a quick chat or call.

We can also use tools like Slack or Zoom to have video or voice chats with them. These tools allow us to see and hear our co-workers, which can help build rapport and trust.

## Be Mindful

While some co-workers may stretch their working time to respond to emails, receive calls and join in on chats, others may not be able to do so. We should be mindful of this and refrain from bombarding them with messages or expecting an instant response. While others accept overtime work errands, others simply can't due to several reasons. We should also be mindful of the time of day we are sending messages. For example, if we know our colleague is asleep, it may not be wise to send a message at midnight.

We should also try to minimize distractions and give our co-workers our full attention when we are chatting or talking on the phone. This will help ensure that we are able to understand them as they understand us. It is a form of respect that we give our full attention to when we are speaking with our co-workers on whatever platform it is.

## Be Open but Respectful

Speak up boldly about your thoughts and ideas, but always be respectful of our colleagues. We should avoid speaking negatively about them or their work and instead, find the good in what they are doing. Constructive feedback can be welcome, but make sure it's given in a constructive way.

Request and suggest in a manner that is respectful. If we have an idea that we think can improve our co-worker's work, we should make a suggestion in a way that is polite and respectful. We should avoid being bossy or demanding and instead, make sure our requests are made in a way that shows we are working together to achieve a common goal.

If we can keep these things in mind, we can successfully maintain healthy relationships with our remote co-workers, regardless of the distance between us.

# How to Communicate Effectively in a Virtual Team

In a world where more and more businesses are becoming remote, communication becomes a key factor in success. When team members are scattered in different cities, states, or even other parts of the globe, it is essential to have a communication strategy that will help everyone stay on the same page.

Though it seems easier to say than to do, there is no doubt that communication is key in a remote team.

Collaboration is the essence of a team. Without proper and effective communication, collaboration is hindered, which can lead to negative outcomes.

In the same sense that office set-up communication is important, remote team communication is just as essential.

# Consensus in Default Tools

In order to have an effective remote communication strategy, team members must be clear on their expectations for communication. Each member of the must be given a chance to voice out what type of communication works best for them.

As a freelancer or entrepreneur, make sure you establish what type of communication you offer, how often, etc. And be open to client preferences! Part of taking on a project may also mean taking on daily communication; if you are adamantly opposed to a client's preferred communication, then this client may be one that you have to pass on.

Each individual in the remote team should have a chance to share what works best for them when it comes to communication. Too often, remote teams default to the easiest form of communication, which is messaging or email. While email is a great way to send documents and keep track of conversations, it can be easily misunderstood if not used correctly.

Chat software, such as Slack, is great for team communication because it allows for both text and voice chat, and files can be easily shared. It is also important to have regular check-ins with remote team members. This could be in the form of a video call, or even just a quick call to see how they are doing. Regular check-ins with remote team members help to build trust and keep everyone on track.

When working with a remote team, it is important to be clear on the expectations for communication.

## Scheduling makes the remote team abide

Remote team communication should be regular and consistent. This means setting a schedule for check-ins and holding people accountable. The remote team leader may devise a plan for communication, but it is essential that team members buy into the plan and are willing to follow it. If team members aren't clear on what is expected of them, or they feel like they can't keep up with the communication schedule, they will likely fall behind in their work.

A remote team should have a communication strategy that works for everyone. A timetable that includes schedules of submissions and check-ins will help to keep everyone on track. Deadlines, due dates, and anticipated meetings should be put in place to help the remote teamwork cohesively.It is also important that the remote team leader be clear on what they expect from their team and hold people accountable.

## Graphics make it simpler

Use visual aids whenever possible. Charts, graphs, screenshots, and videos can be very helpful when trying to explain something complex. For clients, having a portfolio of work or examples can excite them about the finished product they're investing in! In order to avoid any miscommunication, remote team leaders should use visuals as often as possible when explaining something to their team. This will help everyone on the team better understand what is being asked of them, and it can also help with problem-solving.

# Technology should be used effectively

The convenience new technologies offer us can be a curse as well as a blessing.

While new technologies can be a great way for team members to stay connected, they can also be a distraction if not used correctly.

Team members should be encouraged to use technology to their advantage. For example, if someone is stuck on a problem, they can reach out to a team member through chat software or video call for help. When used correctly, technology can be an extremely helpful tool for communication within a remote team. Conference calls or video meetings should be periodically mandatory for all remote teams. This gives everyone the opportunity to hear each other's voices and see each other's faces. It also allows for team members to ask questions and share ideas.

This doesn't mean that each team will be productive with a daily stand-up. However, it can change the dynamic of a team when you have a weekly social where you see everyone's face and listen to people's voices. It brings back the human connection that can get lost over technology.

## Working from Home with a Family or Partner

"Challenging but rewarding" are words that can describe working from home with a family or a partner. It can be a daunting task to try and get work done while caring for loved ones or managing a household, but it can also be extremely gratifying. Ryan works at home with her partner, but their schedules are different. While Ryan is a freelancer who works with multiple clients at a time, Ryan's partner works a traditional job remotely, needing to be logged in from 8 A.M. to 4 P.M.

If you're considering working from home with a family or partner, it's important to be prepared for the challenges that may come up. You have to juggle your work and personal life and find time for both. By being aware of the potential difficulties, you can turn those challenges into triumphs and set yourself up for success. Working from home can be a great way to spend more time with your family or partner. However, it can also be a great challenge. If you live with others, it can be hard to find time and space to focus on your work. You may also have to deal with distractions and interruptions from your loved ones.

If you have young children, it can be hard to find time to work during the day. You may need to get creative with your schedule and find ways to work around your family's daily routine. This will help you to focus on your work when you need to.

One of the trade-offs of working from home is that you may miss out on important family time such as meals or quality time together. Some work schedule requires you to work during non-traditional hours. You may also need to travel for work, which can take you away from your family. You may need to be intentional about carving out time for your loved ones.

It can be difficult to find a balance between work and life when you're working from home with your family or partner. You may find yourself working longer hours or skipping breaks in order to get your work done. You may need to set some boundaries between work time and personal time. Those challenges may be upsetting, but with some trial and error, you'll get it.

Time management is a very crucial aspect when working from home with a family or partner. Tasks can consume your entire day when you are working from home. This can lead to burnout and conflict with your family or partner. Try your best to stick to a schedule as it will help you balance your work and personal life.

Having an organized task schedule can give you more time to enjoy your family or partner. It can be helpful to create a daily or weekly schedule that includes both work and personal time. This will help you make the most of your time and avoid conflict with your loved ones. Make sure to include breaks, meals, and quality time in your schedule. Sticking to routines can help you stay on track when working from home with a family or partner. Having a set schedule for work and personal time will help you balance your responsibilities. Try to stick to a regular sleep schedule, wake up at the same time each day and take breaks at the same times. This will help you in striking a good work-life balance.

Maximizing the technology at your disposal will help you maintain a better work-life balance. You can use alarms or timers to remind you when it's time to take a break or stop working for the day. Use your breaks to spend time with your family or partner. Take a few minutes to chat with them, play with your kids or go for a walk together. This will help you stay connected.

**Communication is the key in any relationship.**

Open communication will help you maintain a healthy relationship with your family or partner. Discuss your work schedules and expectations with each other. This will help you avoid conflicts and set boundaries between work time and personal time. Let them know what you need from them in order to be successful.

Whenever you're feeling overwhelmed or stressed, talk to your loved ones about it. Remember that you have someone to talk to. It's easy to feel isolated while you're working from home. However, you have your family or partner right there with you. Use this as an opportunity to connect with them and build stronger relationships. Spending quality time with them during your break time will strengthen the bond you have as a family or partner.

Communication is not about speaking but also about listening. Make sure to listen to your family or partner when they're talking to you. This will help you understand their needs and concerns. It's important to remember that they are your support system. They want to help you succeed in your work and in life. Another key to communication is to be respectful of each other's time and space. If you need to focus on work, let them know and ask for their understanding.

Know your family members' or partners' love language. Each person expresses and receives love differently. It can be acts of service, words of affirmation, quality time, touch, or gifts. By knowing this, you can show your loved ones that you care about them in a way that they will understand and appreciate. With this, you can better communicate with them which will help you avoid misunderstandings and conflict.

Here are some examples of how you can express your love with different love languages:

- Acts of service: Doing things that your loved ones need or want without them having to ask. This can be making dinner, doing the grocery shopping, taking the dog for a walk, or folding their laundry.

- Words of affirmation: Verbalize your love and appreciation for your loved ones. "I adore you," "thank you for everything you do," or "you're incredible" are examples of phrases to use.

- Quality time: Giving your undivided attention to your loved ones. This can be spending time talking, playing games together, or going on a date night.

- Touch: Physical touch that is appropriate for the relationship. This can be hugs, hand-holding, or cuddling.

- Gifts: Giving gifts that are thoughtful and meaningful. This can be buying your partner their favorite flowers, getting your child a toy they've been wanting, or making a homemade card.

Having your loved ones around you is an inspiration that you can use to strive more while you are working from home. Yes, working from home with a family or a partner can be challenging but can also be a rewarding experience.

# Chapter Eight Action Steps

- How can you intentionally connect with...

  - Co-workers/collaborators?

  - Managers?

  - Clients?

  - Other freelancers?

- How can you maintain healthy family relationships while working from home?

  - If you both work at home, will you work in the same space or different spaces?

  - What will the expectations be around your schedules?

  - Will you have lunch together?

  - Will you log off at the same time?

  - How will you split childcare?

  - How will you tackle housekeeping and meals?

# 9

## BUILDING A HEALTHY WORK LIFE BALANCE

I t was only two months into starting her own therapy practice online, and Susan was burnt out. She found herself working twelve- fourteen hour days, over the weekends, and even at her kid's sporting events. When she started waking up at night and responding to emails, she knew something had to change. Although she loved her work and helping people, her life was desperately out of balance. Anxiety and depression were sneaking in, and Susan began believing that she wasn't cut out for the freelance life after all. Her dream of starting her own online therapy practice was unsustainable.

She went to lunch with an old friend and sobbed about work taking over her life. This isn't what she signed up for; all she wanted to do was help people. Her friend shared with her, "Susan, it's not the business. It's your time management. You need a system that works for your life and business..."

One of the best things about joining the freelance or entrepreneur movement is the ability to control your own time. YOU set the hours of your business, YOU work when you want to, and YOU are the boss. Unfortunately, some freelancers take that to mean you need to be working twenty-four hours a day-in which case, you will quickly burn out.

## Maintaining a Healthy Work-Life Balance While Working Remotely

I saved the best for last. In our final chapter, we are going to revisit the idea of work-life balance. We touched on this briefly when we discussed creating your schedule, but in this chapter, we will dive a bit deeper.

Many virtual workers experience negative effects of working remotely, such as feelings of isolation, less productivity, and difficulty disconnecting from work (like Susan). These difficulties disrupt the balance in an individual's life, preventing them from enjoying quality personal time and rest. If not addressed, this can lead to more significant health consequences like anxiety, depression, and worsening physical health.

Others may experience a different set of issues, such as work overload and the inability to put work away. Especially if they cannot manage their time well, they may feel pressured and stressed while working remotely, leading to frustration, exhaustion, and mental health struggles.

# Is work-life balance a myth?

A healthy work-life may differ in definition from person to person. However, it generally means achieving a balance between work and the other aspects of life such as family, friends, leisure, and health. This does not mean that you are giving exact equal time to each but instead investing as much time in your personal life as you are in your work life.

Understanding the relevance of a balanced work-life is essential for those working remotely. It is important to note that this balance cannot be reached without effort and continuous practice. And, it is going to look different for everyone! Some workers need more downtime than others, some workers need downtime at different parts of the day, and some workers need a lot of variety in both work and life so as not to get the doldrums. Be open to the fact that your work-life balance is going to look different than Jon's, Ryan's, or Susan's.

Ready to talk about your schedule again? Man, it is SO IM-PORTANT!

First, prioritize your time and activities. Before we go any further- how are you going to organize this? Are you going to look at a month at a time? A week? A quarter?

Kristen, a freelance copywriter who is also working on writing her first novel, schedules a month at a time. She gets out her planner and enters all the important non-work items first. Date nights with her husband, a cousin's baby shower, and a writing retreat all go onto her calendar. She gives her first sched-uling priorities to her family, friends, and other activities. We often forget to do this because we get too caught up in work. Understand that your job is not the only thing in your life. Interaction with the most important people in your life should not be sacrificed.

Once she has put in the important life dates, she adds in exer-cise. Kristen recharges her batteries by taking a fun weight-lift-ing class three times a week, running on the treadmill, and walking her dog daily. These all go onto the calendar next. She maintains that she wouldn't be as focused at work and write as brilliantly as she does without incorporating movement into her life. Sitting in front of computers for long hours can take a toll on our physical and mental health. A break is necessary to move around, walk, or do exercises. Working in the comfort of our desks or rooms leaves us more susceptible to unhealthy snacking that can impact our weight.

Finally, she adds in work-client meetings, project due dates, collaboration sessions with other virtual workers, and small business networking events that she attends.

Once she has her calendar outlined, Krista pays special atten-tion to days when she has multiple things going on and days when she has more flexibility. Then, when planning her actual sit-down-at-the-desk-and-write-time, she knows when she has to work ahead on projects because she will be busy later in the week, when she has more downtime to devote to her husband

and extended family, and other odds and ends that are a part of everyday life.

Kristen even goes as far as to pencil in breaks throughout the day to recharge and de-stress. Sometimes she'll go on a quick walk; other times she'll do a bit of cleaning to move her body or drive to the library to get out of the house a bit. This is perhaps one of the most important tips for maintaining a healthy work-life balance. Give yourself enough time to rest and relax to return to work feeling refreshed and with a clear mind. DO NOT plan on sitting in front of the computer for ten hours straight as a freelancer- that is a recipe for failure.

Don't ever feel guilty about spending time on yourself and the things that you enjoy. This is not to say that work is unimportant and should be neglected. However, remember that your job is not the only thing in your life. You deserve to spend time doing what you love, even if it's just for a few hours every week.

Seek support from a mental health professional if necessary. While mental health stigma is slowly dissipating, some people are still apprehensive about seeking help. If you are struggling to cope with work-life balance, talking to someone can help ease the burden that you may be feeling. As for opening up about your mental state to an expert, it is crucial to remember that they are there to help you. They will not judge you for what you are going through and provide the guidance and support needed to overcome it.

It is challenging to establish and maintain a healthy work-life balance, but with proper support, effort, and practice, you can achieve a healthy work-life balance and enjoy the life you have outside of work.

## Setting Boundaries Around Work and Life

To stay productive and sane, it is essential to set boundaries. This can look like closing your office door while you are working or going to your "work spot" in the house, putting your phone across the room so that you're not distracted by personal calls or texts will in the workflow, deleting your work email from your phone (so you only see work email when you log in during work hours), getting several hours before your kids so that you can have quiet, uninterrupted time to work (and going to be early), having a "set" worktime as you would with a normal 9-5 job where your family and friends know you're unavailable, etc. You need to come up with the boundaries that are going to benefit you and be proactive and productive for you as a freelancer.

Take proactive measures to avoid distractions, such as removing social media and email notifications while working. With our work communicated through these channels, it can be tempting to check them frequently. We can avoid the urge to scroll through our feeds and reply to messages during work by silencing notifications.

We may also schedule notifications for the times we want to be alerted to stay focused on our work. After work hours, we may pick up our phone and dedicate a separate device for work, putting it on silent and out of sight. This way, we can balance our time more effectively and ensure that we have enough downtime after our work is done. Devices and accounts used for work can be disabled or deleted when we are not using them.

Jon and Ryan, who are both prone to overwork, created end-of-the-work-day rituals that signal to their brains that work is winding down for the day. Ryan reads and responds to all of her emails as well as writes client updates at the end of the day. She finds this task relaxing and easy, and a good way to end the day. Jon ends his day by writing a to-do list for tomorrow. This gives him a chance to dump all the thoughts that he is left with at the end of the day down before logging out and also gives him a place to start the next morning when he sits down.

What could you do as an end-of-the-work-day ritual? This will help you relax and recharge to show up fully for work the next morning, without going the rest of the evening with work thoughts hanging over your head. When we take care of ourselves, we can be more productive and focused at work.

Use tools and technologies that can help you manage your time more effectively, such as calendar and task management apps. Keeping track of our commitments in one place can help us better manage our time. Some apps can block distracting websites or limit the amount of time we spend on them. Make sure not to mix up your social accounts with work accounts to avoid distractions.

Set alarms and notifications when to stop working and take a break. Some apps may also provide us with statistics on the amount of time spent working. By taking active measures to break up our workday, we can avoid working long hours without rest. This can help us stay on track with our work and avoid burnout.

Seek support from your family and friends, who can help you maintain a healthy work-life balance while working remotely. Aside from making an effort to reach out to others, it is also essential to involve them in our decision-making. This way, we can get their support and buy-in for the changes we want to make in our life.

Keeping ourselves vocal about our work-life balance struggles can also be a powerful way to encourage the necessary changes. Speak when you feel overwhelmed, and be honest about the sustainability of your current work arrangement. Ask for counsel from others, like a trusted friend or family member.

Find what works for you and stick to it through small changes that can lead to a healthier work-life balance over time.

The keys to achieving a healthy work-life balance while working remotely are prioritizing your personal needs, taking measures to avoid distractions, and seeking support from others. By making time for yourself and your interests outside of work, setting boundaries with your devices and accounts, and reaching out to others for support, you can create a sustainable work-life balance over time.

## Not an Empty Cup

As they say, "You can't pour from an empty cup."

To be productive and focused at work, we need to care for ourselves. This means making time for our personal needs, such as relaxation and recreation. With these, we can avoid burnout and focus better on our work.

## Chapter Nine Action Steps

- What does balance look like for you?

- What steps will you put into place to ensure you don't burn out?

- How will you rest and recharge your batteries?

  - When will you exercise?

  - Engage in hobbies?

  - Spend time with family?

  - Take time for yourself?

- What is the maximum amount of hours you are willing to work a week?

- What is the minimum amount of hours you are willing to work a week?

- What do work and family balance look like?

# 10

— ◦ —

## FREQUENTLY ASKED QUESTIONS ABOUT REMOTE WORK

Working from home seems like a dream come true to many people. You are free to wear whatever you like, take as many breaks as you want, and work at your own pace. But is it as great as it seems?

Remote work arrangements nowadays have become more of a norm rather than an exception. With the technological advances that we have and the internet being widely available, companies are now more open to the idea of their employees working remotely.

There has been a recent surge in the number of people working from home. Many people are now in a distance working arrangement, either full-time or part-time or as a freelancer. This can be attributed to the many benefits that come with it, such as increased productivity and flexibility. While there are many benefits to this arrangement, it can also be challenging in some ways.

## FAQs

There are many misconceptions about working from home and it is vital to understand what it entails. Here are some of the most frequently asked questions about working from home:

**Q: What are some of the advantages of working from home?**

A: One of the main benefits of working from home is that it can help to boost your productivity. When you're not commuting and you have a more flexible schedule, you can use that extra time to get more work done. Additionally, working from home can also help you to save money on things like transportation and childcare.

**Q: What are some of the difficulties associated with working from home?**

A: One challenge of working from home is that it can be difficult to stay focused and motivated. When you're not in an office setting, it's easy to get distracted by things like household chores or browsing the internet. Additionally, working from home can also be lonely, as you're not interacting with colleagues regularly.

**Q: How can I overcome the challenges of working from home?**

A: One way to overcome the challenges of working from home is to set up a dedicated workspace in your home. This will help you to stay focused and motivated, as you'll be in an environment that's specifically for work. Additionally, try to schedule breaks throughout the day so that you can take a walk or talk to a friend.

**Q: How can I be productive when working from home?**

A: There are a few things you can do to be productive when working from home. First, set up a dedicated workspace in your home so that you can stay focused. Additionally, try to stick to a regular schedule and take breaks throughout the day. And lastly, make sure to communicate with your team regularly so that everyone is on the same page.

**Q: What if I don't have enough space at home for a dedicated workspace?**

A: If you don't have enough space at home for a dedicated workspace, you can try working at a coffee shop or library instead. Be in an environment that's specifically for work. And lastly, make sure to set realistic expectations for yourself and communicate with your team regularly.

**Q: How can I stay organized when working from home?**

A: One way to stay organized when working from home is to create a daily or weekly schedule. This will help you to keep track of your tasks and deadlines. Additionally, try to set up a dedicated workspace in your home so that you can have a specific place for all of your work materials.

**Q: What are some tips for staying motivated when working from home?**

A: One tip for staying motivated when working from home is to set goals for yourself. This will help you to stay on track and focused on your work. Additionally, make sure to schedule time for socializing so that you don't feel isolated. And lastly, make sure to reward yourself for completing tasks so that you stay motivated.

**Q: What should I do if I start overwhelmed or burned out?**

A: If you start feeling overwhelmed or burned out, it's important to take a step back and reassess your situation. First, try to figure out what's causing you to feel that way. Is it a certain task or project? Is it a specific deadline? Once you identify the cause, try to come up with a plan to make it more manageable. For example, if you're feeling overwhelmed by a project, break it down into smaller tasks that you can complete one at a time.

**Q: What are some tips for staying healthy when working from home?**

A: Some tips for staying healthy when working from home include eating healthy meals, exercising regularly, and getting enough sleep. Additionally, try to take breaks throughout the day to move your body and get some fresh air. And lastly, make sure to schedule time for socializing so that you don't feel isolated.

**Q: What are some remote working etiquette tips?**

A: Some remote working etiquette tips include being respectful of others' time, communicating clearly and concisely, and being proactive. Additionally, make sure to set realistic expectations for yourself and communicate with your team regularly. And lastly, be flexible and adaptable as things change.

**Q: I'm having trouble balancing work and home life. What can I do?**

A: If you're having trouble balancing work and home life, it's important to set boundaries. First, try to stick to a regular schedule. This will help you to have some structure in your day. Additionally, make sure to take breaks throughout the day and schedule time for your personal life. And lastly, be flexible and adaptable as things change.

**Q: Any other advice for working from home?**

A: A few other pieces of advice for working from home include being patient, staying organized, and communicating regularly. Additionally, make sure to set realistic expectations for yourself and your team. Finally, be adaptable and flexible as circumstances evolve.

As more and more people are working from home, it is important to be aware of the pros and cons of this type of work arrangement. There are many benefits to working from home, but there are also some potential drawbacks. Although some challenges come with working from home, the pros outweigh the cons.

# THE COMPLETE CHEAT SHEET TO REMOTE WORK

# Step One

### Before You Go Remote...

1. Secure all the equipment and utilities necessary for remote work.

   - Reliable internet

   - A laptop

   - A GSuite account or Microsoft Office alternative

   - A printer if working with physical documents

   - Headphones (noice-canceling if working around others)

   - Ergonomic mouse and keyboard

2. An home office setup that includes the following:

   - A designated workspace

   - Desk (standing desks are amazing)

   - Notebooks, peens, highlighters, post-it notes

   - A bookcase or storage bin to keep your place tidy

# Step Two

**Transitioning to Remote Work (if you have a traditional job)**

1. Write a proposal to your manager outlining why remote work would benefit the company:

   ○ What your remote hours will be

   ○ Why and how you will be more productive (less distractions, etc.)

   ○ How you plan on being available to your team

   ○ How the company will save money if you work from home

**Transitioning to Remote Work (if you are going to be a freelancer or start your own business)**

1. Build up a savings account with six months - a year of savings for bills

2. Start networking with potential clients

3. Take any classes you need to brush up on skills or change careers

4. Write a rough draft business plan

5. Open a business bank account

6. Determine where, when, how you will get clients

7. Start working on your business website

8. Familiarize yourself with freelance platforms

# Step Three

## Setup Your Home Office

1. Do you have a separate room available for an office?

   - If not, where can you set up to be away from distractions?

2. How will you arrange your home office or area for maximum productivity?

   - Will you be hear a window?

   - Is there wall space for your calendar, diploma, etc.

   - Is there good ventilation?

   - Will you be able to hear and see during meetings?

   - Will you share home office space with a partner or a roommate?

# Step Four

## Making Productivity a Priority

1. Design your work-from-home schedule

   ○ When will you start your morning?

   ○ How will you start your morning?

   ○ What does your midday look like?

   ○ When will you incorporate breaks?

   ○ What days will you schedule meetings?

   ○ How will you end your workday?

2. When is your most productive work time during the day?

   ○ How will you ensure you are working on your top priority during this time?

3. How will you track tasks that need to be completed?

   ○ An online calendar? Planner? Paper calendar?

4. What can you do to prevent procrastination?

   ○ Break down tasks into smaller pieces?

- ○ Reward yourself at the end of a project with some-thing that makes you happy?

- ○ Check in with a co-worker, client, or partner about your progress?

# Step Five

### Building Healthy Relationships

1. Get your family onboard with your remote work plan before going remote

2. Get your partner onboard with your remote work plan before going remote

   ○ Why this will be good for your physical, mental, and emotional health

   ○ How this will give you more flexibility

   ○ Why this is the best option for your family right now

3. Explain to your support system what this is going to look like

   ○ Where your workspace is going to be

   ○ What rules apply when you are working

   ○ How they can best support you

4. Reach out to colleagues about your plan and get their support (also see how you can support them)

# Step Six

## Creating a Work/Life Balance

1. Routines are important!

    ○ Be flexible at first to find what works for you

    ○ Break down your day into morning, midday, after-noon, and evening when planning your routines

    ○ Balance time in front of your computer with time away from the computer

2. Plan family time into your schedule

3. Plan personal time into your schedule

4. Plan exercise into your schedule

5. Plan downtime into your schedule

6. Maximize productivity when working to minimize time working

Made in the USA
Monee, IL
16 November 2022